BELEM

FORTALEZA

RECIFE

SALVADOR

BRASILIA

HORIZONTE

DE JANEIRO

PAULO

ATLANTIC OCEAN

TO ALEGRE

BRAZIL

FLINT RIVER

1996

A Motovun Group Book

© FLINT RIVER PRESS Ltd 1990
2nd, revised edition 1996

Published in the United Kingdom by
Flint River Press Ltd
143-149 Great Portland Street
London W1N 5FB

ISBN 1 871489 05 9

Translator:
Karin Radovanovic

Editor:
Madge Phillips

End-paper design:
Zoran Mujbegovic

Colour separation:
Summerfield Press, Florence

Printed and bound by
Editoriale
Trieste, Italy

CONTENTS

Brazil and the Brazilians
The Rise of Portugal. Ancient Civilizations. Destination - India. First Impressions. Early Colonization. The Jesuit Mission. The Indian Tragedy. The Slave Trade. The White Settlers. The French and the Dutch. Conquest of the Interior.

Land of Promise
Geography. The South - Brazil's Breadbasket. The Dynamic Southeast. The Center-west - A Future in Ranching. The Northeast - Tradition and African Influence. The North - Amazonia. Brasília - Capital of Hope.

From Colony to Republic
Outpost of Empire. The Role of the Church. Era of Expansion. A Nation in the Making. The Paths of Independence. Statehood in Sight. The Imperial Age. The First Republic. The Second Republic. Postwar Progress.

National Goals
Unity and Territorial Integrity. National Integration. Foreign Policy. Democracy. Economic Development.

Religion
Catholicism. Protestantism. Judaism. Afro-Brazilian Cults. Japanese Religions.

Culture
Interwoven Traditions. Literature. Painting. Sculpture. Modern Architecture. Music. Heritage of Mankind.

Life and Leisure
National Characteristics. Food and Drink. Soccer. Carnival. Festival of the Water Goddess.

Distinguished Brazilians
José Bonifácio de Andrada e Silva. José Maria da Silva Paranhos Júnior, Baron do Rio Branco. Getúlio Dornelles Vargas. Juscelino Kubitschek. Joaquim Maria Machado de Assís. Carlos Drummond de Andrade. Antônio Francisco Lisboa-Aleijadinho. Cândido Portinari Torquato. Emiliano August Cavalcanti de Albuquerque Melo. Lúcio Costa. Oscar Niemeyer. Roberto Burle Marx. Heitor Villa Lobos.

Important Dates

Index

BRA

Originated and developed by

NEBOJŠA BATO TOMAŠEVIĆ

Designed by

GANE ALEKSIĆ

ZIL

Text by

VOJISLAV PEKIĆ

Photographs by

JEAN-CHARLES PINHEIRA

FOREWORD

Brazil is a land of superlatives: it is the biggest state of Latin America, of which it occupies forty-seven percent; it has the world's largest river and most extensive tropical rain forests; it is the foremost producer of coffee, sugar and cacao in the world. With its rich diversity of peoples, landscapes, flora and fauna, it may also claim to be the most beautiful and fascinating region on earth, and the one with the greatest potential for economic growth.

This country of continental dimensions, covering 3,286,470 square miles, takes fifth place in the world in size, after the Russian Federation, Canada, China and the U.S.A., and in 1995 was sixth in population after China, India, the U.S.A., Indonesia, and the Russian Federation, with an estimated 155 million inhabitants. Bordering on all the states of South America except Chile and Ecuador, it stretches 2685 miles from north to south, and 2689 miles from east to west. Its Atlantic coastline is 4603 miles long, while its land frontiers have a total length of 9769 miles. Much of the interior is very sparsely populated and offers vast possibilities for new settlement.

Since the very start of European colonization, a unique process of racial intermingling has been a feature of Brazilian life. Unions between whites, Amerindians, blacks, and in the twentieth century Japanese as well, have produced a population with every possible shade of skin color, and, consequently, a high level of racial tolerance. All the races and nationalities integrated in Brazilian society have made some contribution to its culture and way of life, to religion, traditions and customs, to its food, songs and dances.

A land as extensive and fast developing as Brazil inevitably abounds in contrasts and paradoxes: space-age technology coexisting with stone-age tribal life; soaring skyscrapers overlooking squalid shanty-towns (favelas) without running water or electricity; vast natural riches and a huge foreign debt. Dynamic changes in both industry and on the land have accelerated the movement into cities and encourage perpetual migrations in search of work or better pay across the whole territory of Brazil. This acts as an integrating factor, heightening the sense of national identity, of being Brazilian.

The conviction that a country must have self-respect and be true to itself in order to deserve the friendship and respect of the international community was expressed by Brazilian jurist Ruy Barbosa, defending the concept of equality of states and dignity of nations at the Hague Conference of 1907. It is an attitude much fostered in Brazil today.

Despite its present financial difficulties, the Brazilian economy, its sights set on the twenty-first century, has a most impressive list of achievements. In the sphere of industry and mining, it takes second place in the world in production of iron ore, third in aluminium and tin, fourth in gold, steel, manganese, potash and ship-building. In agriculture and livestock production it is the world leader in coffee, sugar and cacao, second in soybeans and orange juice, third in corn (maize), fourth in beef, fifth in cotton... As an exporter of farm produce, it is surpassed only by the United States.

Brazil is a country to which the traveler eagerly returns — drawn by the incomparable panorama of Rio, the lush greenery, the vast expanses, its elegant colonial buildings and stunning modern architecture, the vibrant, colorful life of its cities and, above all, the warmth and spontaneity of its vivacious people.

As far as is possible in one volume, we have tried in words and pictures to convey the feel of Brazil, chart its history, and portray its unsurpassed beauty.

'Chiefs of the Indian Tupinambás Tribe': drawing in the book by the German Hans Staden, 'Two Voyages in Brazil', mid-sixteenth century. Staden spent several months as a prisoner of this tribe.

1.
The Iguaçu Falls, one of Brazil's scenic beauties, are located on the border close to Argentina and Paraguay. The work of millennia, erosion has carved the river bed into hundreds of magnificent cascades.

2, 2a.
The Iguaçu River, after flowing for 609 miles and before meeting up with the Paraná, presents a spectacle of astonishing beauty. The falls, 9000 feet across, are larger even than Niagara or Victoria. ▶ ▶

3.
A tropical sunset near the coastal town of Cachoeira in Bahia state, a region famed for its beauty and balmy climate, its colonial architecture and colorful traditions. ▶ ▶ ▶

4.
A view of Pantanal at sunset. One of the world's largest wildlife sanctuaries, the Pantanal flood plain covers territory in the states of Mato Grosso and Mato Grosso do Sul near the Bolivian border. ▶ ▶ ▶ ▶

5.
Pico de Neblina (Misty Peak) is
Brazil's highest mountain (10,187 ft.).
Located in northern Amazonia, on
the border with Venezuela, Misty
Peak forms part of the mountain
range separating the basins of the
Orinoco in Venezuela and Amazon in
Brazil.

6.
The Chapada dos Guimaraes plateau, an unusual geological formation 41 miles from Cuiabá, capital of Mato Grosso. Many fossils of fish have been found here.

7

7.
A passenger steamer plying the
Amazon. Travel through Amazonia
has always been mainly by water. The
boat trip from Belém to Manaus is an
exciting experience for Brazilian and
foreign tourists alike.

8.
Fishermen returning at the close of
day near Natal, capital of Rio Grande
do Norte. Fishing is a traditional
occupation in northeastern Brazil, a
region famous for its sea food
specialities.

9.
The railroad skirting the slopes of the
Serra do Mar range runs from
Curitiba, capital of Paraná, to the
port of Paranagua. The railroad track
descending from the highlands to the
coast is a remarkable feat of
engineering.

11.
A sailing vessel off the coast of São Luís, capital of Maranhão state in northeastern Brazil. The 'saveiro', as it is called, is used for both fishing and transportation. ▶

12.
The Pioneers, a bronze statue by sculptor Bruno Giorgi on the main square of Brasília. Honoring the pioneers of Brasília, it is considered by many the symbol of the capital. ▶▶

13. ▶▶▶
The church of São João Bosco, dedicated to an Italian saint who in a vision (1883) saw the site of the future capital city. The church has walls of blue stained glass and a glittering crystal chandelier weighing five tons.

10

10.
The Rodovia dos Emigrantes, a modern freeway connecting São Paulo with the port of Santos. Many of the immigrants who came to Brazil from Europe and other countries in the nineteenth and twentieth centuries landed in Santos and found employment in São Paulo. The name of the highway recalls their contribution to the development and prosperity of this great city.

14.
Vale deo Amanhecer (Valley of the Dawn), the center of a sect of mystics, one of several near Brasília, each with its own religious rites and ◀ celebrations.

15.
The weekend handicrafts fair, popularly known as the 'hippie fair', in Brasília. This is the place to find some inexpensive art for a new apartment.

16.
Ver-o-Pezo, meaning 'see the weight', the busiest outdoor market in Belém (Pará). In the photo: juice squeezed from fruit of the Amazon.

17.
With its gleaming new apartment
houses and job opportunities, Brasília
has attracted young people from all
parts of the country, making it the
most truly Brazilian of cities.

19.
The National Theater in Brasília,
designed by Oscar Niemeyer in the
form of an Aztec pyramid.

18.
The J.K. Memorial, dedicated to the
memory of the popular Brazilian
president Juscelino Kubitschek,
builder of the capital. The memorial,
covering 55,000 sq.ft., was designed
by Oscar Niemeyer; the statue in
front is by sculptor Honorio
Pecanha.

20.
Students in front of a telephone
booth. Brazil has a young population,
but the birth rate is now falling.

21.
The cathedral of Brasília, another
masterpiece by Oscar Niemeyer.
Echoing the lines of other buildings
in the capital, this outstanding
example of contemporary religious
architecture achieves an awesome
monumentality. In front of it stands
an impressive composition of the
Four Evangelists.

22

22.
The interior of the cathedral of
Brasília with daylight streaming in
through the glass roof. Ultra-modern
in design, the concrete columns are
suggestive of arms raised in prayer.

23.
The President's Palace (Palácio do Planalto). In the foreground, the façade of the President's Palace, designed by Oscar Niemeyer, and behind it the Congress building. A special attraction for visitors is the Changing of the Guard in front of the palace.

24.
The stone statue of Justice by sculptor Alfredo Ceschiatti in front of the Palace of Justice, i.e. the Federal Supreme Court, another Niemeyer design.

24

25

25.
The Panteão Tancredo Neves, also by
Oscar Niemeyer, was erected after the
ousting of the military regime, in
memory of the tragically deceased
president, Tancredo Neves, and all
who fought for freedom and
democracy in the history of Brazil.

27.
The building of Congress, the
supreme legislative body, is
symbolically the tallest in the capital.
Also symbolically, the main square,
Praça dos Três Poderes, is flanked by
the three buildings of the legislative,
executive and judicial branches.

28.
The Congress building, designed by
Oscar Niemeyer, is the seat of the
House of Deputies and the Senate.
With its semicircular lake and gliding
swans, it is another attraction for
sightseers in the capital. ▶

26.
The austere figure of St. Mark is
often the focal point of snapshots
taken after a visit to the cathedral.

Brazil and the Brazilians

The Rise of Portugal

In the fifteenth century, Portugal, a tiny kingdom on the Atlantic seaboard, relatively isolated from the mainstream of European life but ambitious to develop its trade and political influence, set itself the daunting task of dominating the high seas and creating a worldwide empire.

The Portuguese Court of the time gathered together Europe's finest sailors and cartographers. Under its patronage, the Portuguese designed and built the best ocean-going vessels of the caravel type, improved instruments for navigation, and advanced cartography, giving the western world the science and technology of navigation. They established the geographical latitude as the basis for estimating a vessel's position at sea, and the geographical longitude with the aid of astronomical observations; adapted for use in navigation the astronomer's astrolabe and the quadrant for measuring the altitude of heavenly bodies above the horizon; devised a system of observation that could be used below the Equator, where the pole star, visible only in the northern hemisphere, could not serve as the means for estimating latitude; improved the compass by a system for neutralizing the oscillations caused by a ship's motion, and the sextant, the most practical instrument for determining latitude. In Portugal, cartography became a 'state secret'. One of the oldest sea charts is the Portuguese *Livro de Rotear* (book for navigation), probably dating from the fifteenth century.

All the discoveries in Africa, Asia and South America were soon followed by colonization. Having established its domination on the coasts of Africa, India, Indonesia and China, by the mid-sixteenth century Portugal had gained control over the bulk of trade in precious commodities (gold, ivory, silk, spices and slaves), becoming one of the world's richest imperial powers.

Similar policies of exploration, colonization and domination inevitably led to rivalry and conflict between Portugal and Spain. By the papal bull *Inter caetera*, issued in 1493 by the Spanish-born Pope Alexander VI, Spain tried to secure the territorial advantage. A demarcation line was drawn 100 leagues west of the Azores and Cape Verde Islands, and the Spanish Crown confirmed as the ruler of all lands discovered, or yet to be discovered, west of that line, while Portugal, already holding colonies on the African coast, was to be the sovereign power east of the line. This, the world's first division into spheres of interest, did not satisfy Portugal. Pressure and political activity led to its revision a year later under the Treaty of Tordesilhas: the line of demarcation was shifted to 370 leagues west of Cape Verde, this subsequently giving Portugal the right to claim Brazil, still undiscovered at that time.

Ancient Civilizations

When the Portuguese set foot in Brazil, they found a native population, so-called Indians, of Asiatic origin, whose ancestors had migrated through Siberia and across the Bering Straits to Alaska between 50,000 and 25,000 years B.C. There may also have been some migrations from Polynesia and Australia. Moving slowly southward, these Asiatic peoples reached Central and South America between 15,000 and 10,000 B.C.

Well before the Spanish and Portuguese discovery of the American continent, the Indians of Central America, the Maya, Toltec and Aztec peoples, had developed flourishing civilizations. In South America, the equally advanced Incas dominated almost the entire western coast of the continent. Other groups in South America, among them the tribes settled in Brazil, were primarily nomadic hunters and fishermen, on a far lower civilizational level than the Mayas and Incas with their great cities, sophisticated social and political systems, irrigation schemes and advanced astronomy. Maize (Indian corn) was grown 2500 years B.C. in Mexico, and later joined by other crops: beans, peppers, potatoes...

Early in the first millennium B.C., groups of agriculturalists and potters, probably from the Andean region, settled on the island of Marajó at the mouth of the Amazon.

The people encountered by the Spanish and Portuguese bore some physical resemblance to Asiatics, but their culture had been transformed by adaptation to different environments. The great diversity in language, dress and way of life did not seem to point to a common ancestry.

Destination: India

On March 9, 1500, a fleet of 15 vessels with 1500 men on board set sail for India from the port of Restelo, intending to follow Vasco da Gama's route to India around Africa. This imposing Portuguese expedition, under the command of soldier-diplomat Pedro Álvares Cabral, included cosmographers, Franciscans, merchants, and administrators for Portugal's colonial possessions on the Indian subcontinent. The navigators were the celebrated Bartolomeu Dias, the first captain to round the Cape of Good Hope, and Nicolau Coelho. To avoid the calms of the Gulf of Guinea, the armada sailed so far west that on April 22 the South American mainland was sighted, to be precise, a mountain that was named Monte Pascoal, since it was Easter Day. Cabral promptly claimed the territory for Portugal and called it Santa Cruz, the True Cross, a name soon abandoned in favor of Brazil, after the valuable hard brazilwood (*pau-brasil* in Portuguese), in which the land abounded.

With the fleet anchored half a mile off shore, at the mouth of the river Cai, the Portuguese went ashore for fresh water and made their first contact with the natives. Two days later they sailed northward and dropped anchor in a natural harbor, subsequently named Porto Seguro, in a bay now known as Baia Cabrália, in the southern part of the present federal state of Bahia. That same night, two natives of the Tupiniquin tribe were brought out to Cabral's vessel, returning to shore next day laden with gifts (shirts, red cloth garments, rosaries and small bells). Today, two small towns on the bay, Port Seguro and Santa Cruz de Cabrália, both lay claim to being the place where Cabral first set foot on land and the first Mass was celebrated, on April 26, 1500.

On May 2, one member of the expedition, Gaspar de Lomos, sailed for Lisbon to inform the Portuguese king of this latest addition to his dominions, discovered, it would seem, quite fortuitously. The rest of the fleet resumed the voyage to India, but on May 23, a great storm off the Cape of Good Hope sank four of the ships, among them the vessel captained by Bartolomeu Dias.

First Impressions

There is naturally no way of knowing the size of the native population at the time of the European discovery of Brazil: estimates range from two to five million, who spoke some 300 different languages. Today the figure is between 200,000 and 250,000, speaking about 120 languages. The most important of the tribes encountered by the Portuguese were the Tupi and Guarani. The former lived along the south bank of the Amazon and on the coast, while the Guarani, on a more advanced level of civilization, had their center in what is now Paraguay. The Tupi-Guarani language came to serve as a kind of *lingua franca*: at the end of the eighteenth century it was spoken by some 80 per cent of the Brazilian population. It still survives in some regions of Brazil, and particularly in Paraguay.

According to the earliest Portuguese chronicler, the first Indians, members of the Tupiniquin tribe, greeted the Portuguese on April 24, 1500, with friendly curiosity. He describes them as completely naked red-skinned men and charming young women with flowing black hair, true children of nature in perfect harmony with their environment — a fertile land with abundant rainfall and a pleasant tropical climate.

But the Indians' welcome soon turned to hostility when they realized that the Europeans had come to stay, to seize and exploit the riches of their land and, worst of all, turn them into slaves. In the ensuing struggle to achieve these aims, the native population was enslaved, driven into the interior or slaughtered. Many proud Indians preferred suicide to slavery.

In his book *Two Voyages to Brazil* (1557), the German Hans Staden described the way of life of the Tupi, which, he noted, differed little from that of other tribes. The basic social unit was the hamlet (*aldeia* in Portuguese, *taba* in the Tupi language) consisting of four to seven houses protected by tall fences of palm trunks. In the division of labor, the womenfolk were responsible for sowing, harvesting, gathering fruit and other food, and producing flour, oil, a fermented beverage of boiled manioc, textiles, baskets, pottery and other household articles. The men engaged in hunting and fishing, prepared the ground for cultivation (felling trees, burning and clearing the undergrowth), made canoes, and built houses, which served several families.

The council of elders of the *aldeia*, meeting in the center of the village, decided all matters of common interest, such as the building and site of new settlements and means of defense against enemies. Ties between families were reinforced by the constant exchange of gifts, but this did not prevent their heads from competing for prestige and influence, acquired by possession of a larger number of women (wives, daughters, nieces). The solidarity of the community was reinforced by marriage between families, the undertaking of joint war expeditions, the ritual execution of captured enemies, and periodic collective movement to new territory.

Early Colonization

Thrilled by the news of Cabral's discovery, the Portuguese at once made preparations for further expeditions. The first of these set out in May 1501, under the command of Gaspar de Lomos, and piloted by the famous navigator Amerigo Vespucci, a native of Florence, the only man to have a continent named for him. As the small fleet sailed down the Brazilian coast, Amerigo, calendar in hand, named the places and rivers after the saint who happened to be celebrated on that day. Most of these names (Cape Santo Agostinho, Rio São Francisco and so on) have remained unchanged. On reaching the great Guanabara Bay on New Year's Day 1502, believing it to be the estuary of a large river, he called it Rio de Janeiro (January River).

The first Portuguese expedition had discovered the existence of the valuable brazilwood or red dyewood, much prized on the European market for its hardness and the red or purple textile dye extracted from it. (The Portuguese name, *pau-brasil*, comes from the word *braise*, meaning 'glowing coals' — a reference to its color). This became the first export item of the new colony, providing a rich source of income for the Portuguese Crown, which retained a monopoly on it down to 1859. On the basis of public bidding, the Crown granted concessions to individuals for the exploitation of brazilwood, reserving the right to fix taxes on trading profits. At an auction held as early as 1502, a rich ship-owner, Fernando de Noronha, became the first crown merchant licensed to trade in brazilwood. It was not until 1511, however, that the first cargo of this timber, together with Indians, monkeys and parrots, arrived in Portugal.

In the early days of the colony, the Portuguese were less interested in territorial expansion than in the export of brazilwood, which grew in abundance in the coastal region. Demand for it on the European market lasted for almost three and a half centuries, until the invention of synthetic dyes. In consequence of this lengthy exploitation, in the land which took its name brazilwood is almost unknown today.

The earliest form of Portuguese presence in Brazil was the *feitoria*, a fortified trading post with a garrison of ten to twenty soldiers, of the type already established in the Portuguese colonies in Africa and Asia. Between 1500 and 1530, such posts were founded in half a dozen places to defend Portuguese colonial and trading interests. The latter were not so easily safeguarded. Spanish and French merchant vessels soon appeared on the horizon, bent on preventing the Portuguese from cornering the red-dye market. To frighten off these 'smugglers', Portugal dispatched two 'coast guard' expeditions (1516 and 1526-28). French sources allege that the commander of the second of these ordered the massacre of 300 crew members of confiscated French vessels captured with cargoes of brazilwood in the waters off Bahia.

In the early decades of the sixteenth century, Portugal was more preoccupied with expanding its eastern empire, but Spanish success in extracting gold and silver from Mexico prompted the Crown to pay greater attention to its South American possession. King John (João) III (1521-1577) made the first systematic efforts to establish organized government in Brazil, provide for the territory's defense and encourage settlement. Under the command of Martim Afonso de Sousa, the first real colonizing expedition set sail from Portugal in December 1530. The five vessels carried 400 people (farmers and soldiers), arms, various seeds and livestock. De Sousa, a veteran of European wars and a capable administrator, had the task of applying in Brazil the Portuguese experience gained in colonizing Madeira and the Azores.

For administrative purposes, the coastal region was divided into fifteen districts, hereditary captaincies, conferred by the Crown on nobles and prominent military men known as *donatarios*. Royal charters gave them complete control over their districts and the subjugated population, including the right to levy taxes. Each captaincy comprised 50 leagues of coastline and unlimited territory inland. Contrary to royal expectations, the system proved a dismal failure. Only two of the captaincies flourished: São Vicente, under de Sousa, and Pernambuco. Elsewhere the *donatarios* were incompetent and incapable of protecting the settlements from hostile Indians and French corsairs.

To save the situation, King John eventually decided to establish a single, centralized administration under his direct control. In 1549 he appointed the first governor general, Tomé de Sousa, who had his seat in Salvador (Bahia), the colony's capital down to 1763, when Rio de Janeiro became the seat of government.

Under the new dispensation, the *donatarios* lost their political and judicial powers, but retained their hereditary fiefs until these were taken over by the Crown in the mid-eighteenth century. The towns were placed under municipal governments similar to those in the mother country. These steps intensified the conflict between central government and local interest that was to become a permanent feature of Brazil's colonial history.

The Jesuit Mission

The Catholic Church played a very significant role in the colonization of Brazil, primarily through Jesuit missionaries, who aided this process by converting the natives, settling them in villages (missions), and moving with them into the interior to save them from enslavement. Though their chief concern was to protect the Indians from exploitation, the Jesuits in fact paved the way for Portuguese penetration inland and the expansion of the colony's territory.

With royal approval, the first governor general was accompanied by Manuel de Nóbrega and other Jesuit missionaries, who at once established a school 'for reading and writing' in Salvador (1549). Five years later, on the site of present-day São Paulo, he founded a missionary training school together with José de Anchieta, later known as the 'Apostle of Brazil' for his selfless labors on behalf of the Indians. In the seventeenth century, Father Antonio Vieira set up a chain of missions along the Amazon, to which the Jesuits, by patient persuasion, attracted some 60,000 Indians. Because of constant attacks by the Portuguese settlers, the missionaries supplied the Indians with arms and enabled them to escape into the jungle, whence they followed them. Despite the Jesuits' efforts, in the seventeenth century the colonists forced over 300,000 Indians into slave labor.

The Jesuit activity, fiercely resented by many settlers, was abruptly cut short in 1759 when the powerful Portuguese prime minister, the Marquis of Pombal, angered by their opposition to some of his colonial reforms, ordered the expulsion of all members of the Society of Jesus from both Brazil and Portugal.

The Indian Tragedy

Steadily and ruthlessly deprived of their land, succumbing to European diseases, decimated by wars and reduced to various forms of dependence, the native population dwindled from several millions in 1500 to a mere quarter of a million at the last reckoning. The majority now live in Amazonia and parts of Mato Grosso.

In the colonial period, Portuguese legislators oscillated between the interests of the colonists in need of slave labor for their plantations and mines, and the missionaries, who wanted to make Christian citizens of the Indians. Though the colonial reforms of the Marquis of Pombal gave the Indians legal equality in 1758, in practice their tragedy continued, an inevitability of colonial policy.

After the Portuguese royal family took refuge in Brazil in 1808, fleeing from the Napoleonic invasion, new legislation further exacerbated the position of the native population. The white colonists escalated their struggle for land, while those in the poorer regions, unable to afford African slaves, did their utmost to subjugate the Indians.

The Slave Trade

As early as 1441, trade in African slaves became a highly profitable 'export branch' of Portugal, one in which it led the world for a time. In addition to sales to other countries, slaves were early on used to work the sugar plantations in the Portuguese Atlantic islands.

The first slaves arrived in Brazil in the mid-fifteenth century, and from 1559, at the request of the *donatarios* and settlers, the Crown began to organize trade in slaves for Brazil. Every sugar-cane plantation owner had the right to import 120 slaves from Africa annually.

Historians' estimates of the number shipped to Brazil over the centuries vary widely — from 3.5 to 13 million. What is certain is that by the early nineteenth century, the blacks outnumbered by two to one the rest of the colony's population — whites, Indians and mestizos (persons of mixed white, black and Indian origin). Ethnically, they belonged to several groups: Sudanese, West Sudanese and Bantu.

Black slave labor, vital to the colony's economy, was used on the plantations of sugar-cane, tobacco, coffee and cotton, in the gold and diamond mines, and in domestic service. On the great estates (*fazendas*), living in wretched conditions on a diet of manioc flour, beans and bananas, they toiled from twelve to sixteen hours a day. According to Brazilian historians, their useful working life was only ten to fifteen years, so that the owners, oblivious it seems to cause and effect, exploited them to the maximum for this brief period. "Brazil is sugar, and sugar is the Negro" is how one writer summed it up. By the end of the sixteenth century, sugar production, concentrated in the northeast, had become the mainstay of the colony's prosperity, and remained so for some two centuries. The great *fazendas* in the regions of Bahia and Pernambuco were owned by a relatively few wealthy families who maintained a luxurious life-style. Their huge mansions were crammed with valuable possessions, their horses caparisoned with silver, their wives and daughters dressed in the finest velvets and silks, outdoing the noble ladies of Lisbon, it was said, in vanity and coquetry.

The Africans did not accept their slavery passively. Periodically they rose against their owner, slew him and fled into the forests. The best-known organized rebellions were in Bahia in the first half of the nineteenth century, but major armed uprisings also occurred in Minas Gerais, Maranhão and elsewhere. From the very early days, runaway slaves set up their own settlements (*quilombos*). The most famous of these, in Palmares (now the federal state of Alagôas), lasted almost a century, till its destruction in 1869. This was a confederation of villages with some 20,000 inhabitants. The day of the death of its leader Zumbi (November 20) has been adopted by the contemporary black-rights movement in Brazil as the National Day of Black Consciousness.

The disappearance of slavery was a gradual process, depending on the economic circumstances in the individual provinces. At the end of the colonial period, the slave population mostly consisted of Bantus from Portuguese colonies: Angola, Mozambique and Cabinda. With some prompting from Great Britain, Brazil officially abolished the trade in 1831, but slaves were still bought and sold down to 1853. Finally, in 1888, Princess Isabel, while acting as regent for her father, Emperor Pedro II, during his absence from the country, proclaimed complete abolition. The liberal Pedro II himself declared that he would sooner lose his crown than assent to the continuation of slavery.

The White Settlers

The earliest settlers in Salvador (Bahia) came from southern Portugal with its tradition of large feudal estates. The second group arrived in 1507 in the area of São Vicente, where Martim Afonso de Sousa established the settlement of that name — Brazil's oldest city — in 1532. These settlers, coming from the poorer north of Portugal, maintained good relations with the Tupi-Guarani Indians and, later, with African slaves. In 1554 they founded the first settlement on the site of present-day São Paulo.

The Portuguese who immigrated to Brazil came from various social strata. The nobility (*fidalgos*) and soldiers who had distinguished themselves in the exploration and colonization of Africa and Asia were granted land concessions and formed the highest class in the colony. Next came the Catholic clergy, most notably the Jesuits, who played an important role in organizing society. Then there were the common folk, farmers and craftsmen, the true settlers, who paved the way for the development of Brazil. Among the early white inhabitants were numerous convicts, deported to the colony instead of serving terms of imprisonment or being sent to the galleys.

Drawing on their experience gained in Madeira and the Azores, in fertile Brazil the Portuguese developed a colonial economy based primarily on plantations and slave labor. Along with brazilwood, sugar soon became the colony's main export. The raising of sugar cane, begun in São Vicente and later concentrated in the northeast, was the principal source of the colony's wealth and Crown revenues for some two hundred years. For most of this period, Brazil was the world's largest sugar producer, until the Caribbean plantations, thanks to higher productivity, were able to undercut the price and Brazil's sugar output declined. From the eighteenth century on, other plantation crops — tobacco, cacao and cotton — became increasingly lucrative exports. Plantation ownership concentrated wealth in the hands of a relatively few powerful families and set the colony's socio-economic structure in a mold that has endured into the twentieth century.

The glitter of New World gold must have drawn many of the early settlers to Brazil, but no significant amounts were found until the big strike in the state of Minas Gerais in 1693, followed by major finds in Mato Grosso and Goiás (1725). A hectic gold rush led many thousands of adventurous souls up the São Francisco River into the wilds of the interior. In the eighteenth century, an estimated 1000 tons of gold were extracted, giving an enormous boost to the colony's development. One consequence of the gold rush was the transfer of the capital from Salvador to Rio de Janeiro, closer to the gold fields. In 1729, gold-seekers in Minas Gerais struck extra lucky, discovering a rich diamond field. Others were found shortly after in Bahia and Mato Grosso, prompting the Crown to make diamonds another royal monopoly in 1731. The extraction of gold, diamonds and other gems peaked in the mid-eighteenth century. By its end, the richest gold mines in Minas Gerais (meaning 'general mines') had been worked out, but revenue from diamonds continued to fill the royal coffers.

Coffee, now Brazil's major crop, was something of a latecomer. Introduced in 1727 at Belém, in the state of Pará, it later spread all along the coast from Rio de Janeiro to the Amazon, and after 1825 southward to São Paulo. Since coffee-drinking had become all the rage in eighteenth-century Europe, the demand was enormous, and many Europeans headed for Brazil, hoping to make their fortunes as coffee-growers.

A share of the colony's wealth was, of course, appropriated by the Crown, which took one tenth of the produce of the land it had 'conferred' on the settlers, a fifth of the mining production, and the revenue from some forty taxes.

The French and the Dutch

Portugal did not secure its rich colony without a struggle. As early as 1504, France, which had never accepted the Treaty of Tordesilhas dividing the New World between Spain and Portugal, set its sights on the Brazilian coast, where French merchants, with Indian assistance, loaded their vessels with brazilwood. In 1555, it attempted to establish a colony, named Antarctic France, in Guanabara Bay, as a place of refuge for Huguenots and other Protestants. Five years later, Portuguese troops succeeded in driving them out, and in 1567 the city of Rio de Janeiro was founded there to secure the natural harbor. A subsequent French attempt to found

29.
On the night between December 31 and January 1 the beaches of Rio fill with people observing or taking part in a ceremony honoring the sea goddess, Iemanjá. After prayers, singing and dancing, at midnight boats bearing gifts sail out to sea to 'propitiate' this Afro-Brazilian deity.

30.
A woman holding dolls that she will commit to the waves as a gift for the goddess Iemanjá.

31

31.
Waiting for dawn on a beach in Rio
de Janeiro. Dressed in white, women
toss bouquets of flowers into the sea
for the water goddess.

32.
White is the dominant color in the costumes of the participants, mostly women, but there are also touches of blue, supposedly the favorite color of the sea goddess, and yellow for the god Oxum. Every year more and more people come with gifts for the goddess: cosmetics, perfume, even champagne.

33

34

33.
Baptism in the sea as performed by the Reino de Deus sect at Abaite, Salvador, capital of Bahia.

34.
Flowers, dolls and other offerings to the water goddess floating on the waves near Salvador (Bahia).

35, 36.
The 'washing of the Bomfim', another
water-related ritual, is performed
between January 15 and 17 in
Salvador (Bahia). Though the church
is Catholic, the ceremony is
essentially Afro-Brazilian in origin. It
consists of washing the steps and area
in front of the church of Nosso
Senhor do Bomfim.

37.
Two women dressed in Bahian
costume participate in the Iemanjá
ritual on one of Rio's beaches.

38.
Offering prayers to the sea goddess in
Rio de Janeiro. Elements of
paganism have survived in these
ceremonies celebrated in Rio,
Salvador and other places in
northeastern Brazil.

39

39.
The feast of Our Lord, the patron of sailors (Nosso Senjor dos Navigantes), is marked on January 1 in Salvador (Bahia) by a procession of decorated boats carrying images of Christ, known as the Bon Voyage Festival (Festa da Boa Viagem).

40.
A church procession in the ancient city of Ouro Prêto (Minas Gerais). Various religous traditions and customs have survived from the colonial period. Holy Week, one of the great Catholic feasts, is celebrated by most of the local population.

41

41.
All prepared for the 'washing of the Bomfim', a ceremony which has not always been fully approved by the Catholic clergy.

42.
The Irmandade da Boa Morte
(Sisterhood of the Good Death) at
Cachoeira, near Salvador (Bahia)
have rituals combining elements of
Catholic liturgy with various African
customs. The Irmãs da Boa Morte
are Catholics who usually work as
sisters of charity in hospitals, caring
for patients and easing their last days
on earth.

42

43.
Detail of the Candomblé ritual in Rio
de Janeiro. The members of this
Afro-Brazilian cult believe in
reincarnation of the individual with a
new outlook on life.

43

44.
Irmãs da Boa Morte taking part in a
funeral ceremony in Cachoeira, near
Salvador (Bahia). A wax effigy
representing the deceased, but
resembling the Virgin Mary, is placed
on the coffin.

45.
Irmã da Boa Morte bearing a candle
at a funeral in Cachoeira.

the colony of Equatorial France in the present state of Mananhão was likewise doomed to failure. A Portuguese land and sea blockade forced the French to surrender in 1615 and finally abandon their Brazilian aspirations.

In 1580, when the Spanish king imposed his claim by inheritance to the Portuguese throne, Portugal's colonial possessions came under attack from Spain's enemies, notably Holland, a rival sea-power that had recently gained its independence. To protect its sugar trade, Holland began the 'sugar war' against the northeast coast of Brazil (Bahia and Pernambuco), capturing Salvador (Bahia) in 1624, but being compelled to withdraw a year later.

In 1630 a fleet sent by the Dutch West Indies Company took Recife in the state of Pernambuco, the main center of sugar production, where the Dutch remained for twenty-four years. During the governorship of the capable and enlightened Prince Maurice of Nassau, the city flourished and sugar production was reorganized and modernized. Eventually, in 1654, Portuguese-Spanish troops forced the Dutch to surrender, and Holland subsequently relinquished all claims to Brazil.

Conquest of the Interior

In the period of colonization, the relatively small population of Brazil was concentrated in the narrow coastal belt, where Portuguese aristocrats held huge estates, worked by slaves. Until the early nineteenth century, the only inland areas where white settlers had penetrated in any numbers were in the states of São Paulo and Minas Gerais. The decision to build a new capital, Brasília, in the heart of the country was a symbolic act of faith in the future of the vast interior of the land, a bold and far-sighted attempt to draw the population away from the coast towards the undeveloped and almost uninhabited central and western plateaux.

A major role in opening up the interior was played by organized expeditions (*bandeiras*) into the present states of Minas Gerais, Goiás and Mato Grosso in search of Indian slaves and, later, mineral wealth. Each with its own flag (hence the name *bandeira*), these expeditions claimed about two thirds of Brazil's present territory for the Portuguese Crown. Most set off from São Paulo, a region whose inhabitants, known as Paulistas, were noted for their toughness. This quality was certainly essential during these treks into the uncharted wilderness, sometimes lasting years, on which whole families sometimes went along, intending to settle in the new regions. In this respect the *bandeiras* were similar to the movement westward in the pioneering days of North America.

Pressing westward, the colonists had, in fact, overstepped the mark — the demarcation line of Spanish-Portuguese spheres of interest dating from the Treaty of Tordesilhas. In 1750, the two Iberian kingdoms reached an agreement whereby the treaty was annulled and the territory of Brazil was to extend from the Amazon in the north, as far west as the Andes and south to the Rio la Plata.

46.
A woman in the traditional costume of Bahia preparing for the festival of the sea goddess held annually at Salvador (Bahia). The worship of river deities in Africa has been transferred in Brazil to the sea. Iemanjá is venerated as the supreme deity, mother of the gods.

One of the earliest drawings of the
people of the New World, Indians of
Brazil, published 1505.

Land of Promise

Geography

Geographical and climatic factors exerted a major influence on the history and development of Brazil. With its long Atlantic coastline (4603 miles) it lay open to Portuguese, Spanish, French, Dutch and English colonizers. In the period of colonization, it became famous for its timber (brazilwood), sugar, gold, diamonds, cotton, tobacco, cacao, coffee, and rubber.

Topographically, Brazil can be divided into five zones.

In the north the Guiana Highlands, partly forested, form a natural boundary with northern neighbors and divide the watershed of the Orinoco River in Venezuela from the vast Amazon basin. Here, close to the Venezuelan border, rises Brazil's highest mountain, Pico de Neblina (Misty Peak, 10,187 ft.).

The Amazon basin in the northern and western regions, drained by the world's largest river and its many great tributaries, occupies more than a third of Brazilian territory. In its upper part lies the country's most extensive plain, mostly less than 800 feet above sea level, covered by tropical rain forest.

The Brazilian Highlands, between the Amazon in the north and the Rio la Plata in the south, have plateaux ranging from 3000 to 4000 feet in altitude. The highest mountain in the south is the Pico da Bandeira (Flag Peak, 9,511 ft.). The eastern margin of the Highlands, known as the Great Escarpment, follows the Atlantic coastline from Salvador (Bahia) to Pôrto Alegre, in places rising almost sheer from the sea to a height of 2600 feet and making access to the interior difficult.

The watershed to the Rio la Plata in the south has a variety of terrain — highlands, forests and tall-grass prairie (pampas), a higher altitude than the Amazon basin and a cooler climate.

The coastal zone, varying in width, is of exceptional importance: forming only 7.7 percent of the national territory, it has 30 percent of the total population.

Brazil's enormous economic potential certainly owes much to its great inland waterways, which form three major river systems. The mighty Amazon, the world's biggest river in volume of water, with over 1000 tributaries, flows through Brazil for 1985 of its total 4362 miles. It is navigable for much of its course through Brazil. The Paraguay-Paraná-La Plata system drains most of the southern part of the country. The Paraná, the third largest river in Brazil, is navigable for some 340 miles. The third major system is that of the Rio São Francisco, second in size to the Amazon but the largest wholly Brazilian river, famed for its spectacular waterfalls with vast hydroelectric potential.

Though mainly within the tropics, most of Brazil is blessed with a pleasant, moderate climate, without great extremes of temperature or rainfall. Even in the Amazon basin on the Equator, the temperature averages only 80°F and never exceeds 96°F. Along the coast, from Recife to Rio de Janeiro, the annual mean ranges from 73° to 80°F. Snow and frost occur in the south and southeast, where the mean temperature is 62° to 66°F. The rainy season in the south is from December to March. Humidity is relatively high, especially along the coast.

Brazil is the size of a continent. Several of its federal states are exceptionally large: Amazonia, for example, is bigger than Alaska, more than twice the size of Texas and three times the size of France; the state of Mato Grosso exceeds the combined areas of France, West Germany, the Netherlands and Belgium.

On the basis of geographic, economic, cultural and social differences, this immense territory can be subdivided into five major regions. The *South*, where European immigrants have left the strongest imprint, is the most important for agriculture. The *Southeast* is the economic, cultural, scientific and technological center. The *Center-west*, with its vast expanses of grazing land, is foremost in ranching. The *Northeast* is a true reflection of Brazilian tradition and the African influence, while the *North* characterized by its great river system and the world's largest tropical rain forests, is the last outpost of the Amerindians. Just traveling across this land of gigantic proportions, from south to north, from east to west, is a feat in itself.

The South - Brazil's Breadbasket

Comprising the federal states of Rio Grande do Sul, Santa Catarina and Paraná, this region is the smallest in size — slightly less in area than the Iberian Peninsula. The only part of Brazil south of the Tropic of Capricorn, it has a predominantly subtropical climate with four seasons, which made it the most attractive for European immigrants.

In the highlands there are coniferous forests with the well-known Paraná pine, now fast disappearing, and on the grassy pampas an evergreen shrub called maté, from which a kind of tea is made. This is a favorite thirst-quencher of the gauchos, who carry it in a special maté gourd. Brazil has hundreds of plants with medicinal properties, discovered by the Indians, which are still used, sometimes very effectively, to cure various diseases. The originally luxuriant vegetation has been seriously endangered, primarily by the cutting of forests, and in the north, by erosion.

In the official report submitted by Pero Vaz de Caminha to the king of Portugal after the discovery of Brazil, the colony was described as a land of aromatic plants and tall trees. Clearly the Portuguese conquistadores and later generations of settlers did not have the same admiration for Brazil's flora: the forest cover of the Atlantic seaboard, known as Mata Atlântica, which it had taken from 12,000 to a million years to create, was obliterated in less that five centuries. Thus, the inhabitants of Brazil destroyed one of their greatest heritages, permitting the extinction of many species of plant and animal life. When the first Europeans arrived in Brazil the forests of the coastal belt of Rio Grande do Norte and Rio Grande do Sul covered some 135,000 square miles, now reduced to about 3,850 square miles, or three percent of the original forestland.

The steady Portuguese penetration south, north and west inevitably led to conflicts with the Spanish, particularly in the lower reaches of the Rio la Plata. In 1680, on the territory of present-day Uruguay the Portuguese Manuel Lobo founded the colony of Sacramento, later a bone of contention between Portugal and Spain.

In the second half of the seventeenth century the Jesuits established their first villages in the south, which eventually grew into the cities of Rio Grande do Sul. Together with the Indians the missionaries organized the production of wheat, corn, rice, sugar cane, cotton, tobacco and oranges. Cotton and maté were exported to Buenos Aires.

The settlement of the coast of present-day Rio Grande do Sul was completed in the eighteenth century by Portuguese soldiers from the Azores, who also gradually settled the coast of Santa Catarina. As frontier guards with the task of defending the occupied territory against Spanish expeditions, they were granted various privileges and benefits — land, tools, seed grain, livestock. After the expulsion of the Jesuit missionaries in 1759, the Portuguese settlers spread inland, attracted by the livestock that the Jesuits and Indians had abandoned. Unions between the Portuguese from the Azores and native Indians resulted in a typical representative of the region, the gaucho, very similar to the gauchos of Uruguay and Argentina. The Brazilian gaucho has made a distinctive contribution to the country's many-faceted culture: a form of speech mixing the Portuguese and Spanish languages, a pastoral way of life, picturesque costume, ways of cooking, songs and dances.

The South, in general, is considered the 'breadbasket' of Brazil, but Rio Grande do Sul is the land of the gauchos, the 'cowboys' of Brazil. Initially nomads, today farmers and ranchers, they have kept their picturesque costume: wide-brimmed brown hat, baggy trousers (*bombachas*), neck scarf, poncho, and wide leather belt (*guaiaca*). Their gear consists of a lasso for roping cattle, three balls of metal or stone tied to a rope and thrown in front of the cattle to stop them (*boleadeiras*), a special knife attached to the belt for cutting meat and making cigarettes, a belt (*tirador*) to hold the lasso, and a maté gourd (*chimarrao*). Gaucho specialities are charcoal-grilled meat (*churrasco*) and dried meat (*charqueada*).

The gaucho, who developed a specific way of life as a rancher and frontier guard, is inseparable from his horse: he rides so much he is jokingly said to have lost the use of his legs. Every second year, toward the end of January, a famous rodeo is held in the farming town of Vacaria, in Rio Grande do Sul, the biggest event of its kind in South America.

Pôrto Alegre, capital of Rio Grande do Sul, was first settled between 1732 and 1740, when the Portuguese government dispatched fifty couples from the Azores to Pôrto dos Casais ('port of married couples'). In 1824 groups of German settlers and artisans settled in São Leopoldo, north of Pôrto Alegre. During the next twenty-five years the Brazilian government sent over 20,000 German immigrants to the region, where they raised rye, corn and hogs. From here they founded other towns: Teutonia and São Lourenço. Between 1870 and 1890 immigrants from northern Italy arrived in the uplands north of the German settlers and founded the towns of Caxias do Sul, Garibaldi and Santo Bento Gonçalves.

Today Pôrto Alegre is the largest commercial center south of São Paulo, its market said to be a faithful copy of the Mercado da Figueira in Lisbon. In the lower part of the city the street named Travessa dos Venezianos is a picturesque survival of colonial times.

Caxias do Sul is the center of viticulture and host to the Grape Festival from February to March every three years. Vines were introduced from Italy, and soon Italian immigrants were making wine. About 98,800 acres of vineyards in Bento Gonçalves, Garibaldi, Caxias do Sul and Flore da Cunha yield 535,000 tons of grapes a year. Some 24,000 families, all descendants of immigrants from Piedmont, Lombardy and the Veneto, 'live from wine and for wine', as the local saying goes. Today Brazil, along with Chile and Argentina, is a noted producer of fine wines.

In 1822 the present state of Santa Catarina began to be settled by German immigrants, who first founded the town of Blumenau in the interior and then Joinville on the coast. Italian immigrants came later to the valley of the Tijucas and raised the towns of Nova Italia, Nova Trento and others. In 1726 a settlement was established on the site of Florianopolis, the present capital of Santa Catarina, to encourage the population of the southern Brazilian coast.

Italians were the first Europeans to put down roots in the state of Paraná. Most of the later immigrants in the nineteenth and twentieth centuries were of Slav origin: Poles, Russians, Ukranians. After 1860 groups of British farmers began to settle there.

Paraná is Brazil's leading producer of wheat, rye, potatoes and black beans. The capital, Curitiba, is a well-planned modern city, especially the European-style center. Its cathedral on Tiradentes Square was inspired by the famed cathedral of Barcelona. Downtown Curitiba also has a popular public promenade, as well as three theaters. The city grew out of two settlements founded in the mid-seventeenth century by gold-seekers: Nossa Senhora de Luz and Bom Jesus dos Pinhais. When the mines were exhausted, cattle-raising and, later, the export of tea secured Curitiba's continuing prosperity. Coffee production in northern Paraná also contributed notably to the development of the capital: 1940 — 140,000 inhabitants, 1980 — over a million.

The South holds the lead in the production of rice, wheat, corn, soybeans, potatoes and coffee, and ranks second, after the Southeast, in industrial production. The region has huge hydroelectric potential: 23,000 megawatts of electricity from the Paraná river basin. The beautiful Salto de Sete Quedas waterfalls on the Paraná River were regrettably inundated when a power plant of 12,600 MW was built on the Itaipu River. The amount of material used in its construction (13 billion cubic meters) would have built 200 soccer stadiums the size of Rio's Maracanã. Its dam holds back 29 billion cubic meters of water, three times the volume in Guanabara Bay.

One of the country's scenic wonders, the Iguaçu Falls, is located on the border between Brazil, Argentina and Paraguay. The waterfalls, larger than Niagara in the U.S.A., are among the most beautiful in the world.

The Dynamic Southeast

The most important and developed region of Brazil, the Southeast, is the country's political, economic, cultural, scientific and technological center. It comprises the states of Rio de Janeiro, São Paulo, Minas Gerais and Espirito Santo (Minas Gerais alone is bigger than France). Though the region covers only 10.86 percent of the national territory, nearly half of the population of Brazil lives in the Southeast, which has the country's three largest cities: São Paulo — 9.6 million in the metropolitan area, Rio de Janeiro — 5.5 million and Belo Horizonte over two million inhabitants.

Rio de Janeiro was Brazil's capital for almost two centuries (1763-1960) and is still considered the cultural center of the country. Its location makes it one of the most beautiful cities in the world.

São Paulo is today the greatest commercial and financial heart of Brazil and Latin America. The state of São Paulo, with a larger population than Argentina or Columbia, is greater in area than the states of New York and Pennsylvania together, and only slightly smaller than Great Britain.

Belo Horizonte, the first planned city in Brazil, was raised at the very end of the nineteenth century on a site first settled in 1701 by the *bandeirante* João Leite da Silva Ortiz. Modeled after Washington D.C., it was built as the new capital of the state of Minas Gerais, in place of Ouro Prêto, a city in decline which was in any case less accessible and central than Belo Horizonte.

Victória, capital of Espirito Santo, grew out of the settlement, Vila da Nossa Senhora da Victória, founded in 1535 by the *donatario* of Espirito Santo.

Brazil's fastest growing city is São Paulo. By the late Thirties the population of the state of São Paulo numbered a million Italians, half a million Portuguese, half a million settlers from other parts of Brazil, 411,000 Spanish, 200,000 Japanese, etc., all amicably living side by side, an unparalleled example of national and racial integration.

In industrial and technological development São Paulo is definitely Brazil's dynamo. It boasts a higher concentration of West German industrial capital than anywhere else on earth, and after Göteborg and Stockholm is the biggest center of Swedish-owned industry.

Following the American Civil War, between 1866-1867 a number of families, disappointed in its outcome, moved to Brazil and founded the city of Americana not far from Campinas in the state of São Paulo. The first group, numbering about 2070, was led by Colonel William Norris. Immigrants from the states of Alabama, Florida, Louisiana, Mississippi, South Carolina and Virginia, subsequently settled elsewhere in the province of São Paulo, and in Espirito Santo, Rio de Janeiro, Pará, Minas Gerais, Bahia and Pernambuco.

Much earlier, at the beginning of the nineteenth century, a group of Chinese came to the Southeast to work on the tea plantations, under an arrangement made by the Brazilian Ministry of Foreign Affairs, but the experiment was short-lived.

Economic progress was further accelerated once the mountain barrier separating the coast from the interior was overcome thanks to a system of communications linking up the region and connecting it with the Brazilian hinterland. Changes within the region were rapid. On former coffee plantations in the valley of the Paraiba do Sul with the crumbling mansions of the first 'coffee barons' now stand the huge Volta Redonda steel works and the Campos sugar mills.

São Paulo and Rio de Janeiro serve as a kind of barometer measuring Brazil's growth and its future prospects. In São Paulo, the pulsating heart of the country's economy, its inhabitants, Paulistas as they are called, share the enterprise, industry and business acumen of the European and Japanese immigrants who have given the city its cosmopolitan air and quality of life. But it is the inhabitants of Rio de Janeiro, Cariocas, outgoing, cheerful, full of life, who epitomize in a sense the soul of Brazil.

São Paulo and Rio de Janeiro were not bypassed by the urban growth characteristic of postwar Brazil and Latin America. The absence of real agrarian reforms attaching people to the land triggered large-scale migration from country to town, particularly from the interior to the capital cities, and resulted in one of the country's gravest social problems. Millions of impoverished inhabitants live in the *favelas* of Rio de Janeiro, only a stone's throw from luxurious residential quarters, and are part of the daily scene. The bustling city of São Paulo boasts more skyscrapers, factories, scientific institutions. It is known for its International Art Biennial (October-November in odd-number years) and the international São Silvestre Street Race on December 31. Nevertheless, Rio is everyone's favorite. It radiates a spirit of candor, intimacy, high spirits and tolerance. This is the Rio experienced at its big folk festivals: the pre-Lenten carnival, the festivities honoring Iemanjá, mother of the gods, on the night of December 31, and the fantastic soccer matches played at the Maracanã stadium.

Rio, an ancient city by the standards of the southern hemisphere, has much to offer lovers of history and the arts. In the National Library in Rio connoisseurs of the colonial period will find rare manuscripts, the earliest collections from Lisbon. The Brazilian Academy of Letters is a replica of the Petit Trianon in Versailles, presented by the French government for the centenary of Brazilian independence. The National Museum is one of the finest in Latin America; its entrance hall displays the huge Bendego meteorite, found in 1888 in the state of Bahia, believed to be the largest metal mass (about five tons) ever to fall on the earth. The sacristy of the Convent of Santo Antônio, second oldest in the country, contains a relic venerated by women seeking husbands, while its crypt has the tomb of a Scottish officer known as wild Jack of Skelater, in the service of the Portuguese government at the time of the Napoleonic Wars, who became chief of staff of the Portuguese army in Brazil. The monastery of São Bento contains splendid works of art from the seventeenth and eighteenth centuries, especially seventeenth-century Baroque. A masterpiece by the first Brazilian painter, Father Ricardo do Pilar, *The Savior*, hangs in the sacristy. The lovely small church of Nossa Senhora da Glória was a favorite of the imperial family; Emperor Pedro II was baptised there. Its elaborate wooden altar is the work of master carver Valentim, son of a Portuguese aristocrat and an African slave.

Rio's beautiful Botanical Gardens covering 348 acres has 40,000 classified plants, a Garden of Eden featuring 5000 species of flora from five continents. Blossoming in February and March, the giant lily *Victoria regia* begins to open in the afternoon and by night is in full flower, spreading its powerful scent. The first orchids were brought from the Gabrielle Botanical Gardens on the island of Mauritius. The first seeds

48.
Aerial view of Pantanal (Mato Grosso and Mato Grosso do Sul), the flood plain of the upper Rio Paraguay, famed for its extraordinary diversity of flora and fauna. ▶

49.
The last rays of the sun illuminate flocks of birds in Pantanal, the world's largest wildlife refuge. ▶▶

47.
Brazil has many different species of the flat-faced new world monkey, all of them tree-dwellers with long prehensile tails. None of them approach the apes of the old world in size. The biggest is the howler monkey, whose powerful call echoes for miles through the jungle.

50

50.
A capybara moving freely among a
group of birds on the banks of a
Pantanal river. This South American
member of the guinea-pig family is
the largest living rodent, growing four
feet tall and weighing up to 100
pounds in maturity. A shy, gentle
creature, it is an expert swimmer and
diver.

51.
Pantanal's most formidable
inhabitant is the brazilian alligator
(jacaré). Sunning themselves
peacefully on a river bank, they are
totally unaware that ruthless
poachers are eager for their skins.

51

52.
The sloth, found only in tropical America, is a nocturnal creature.

53.
A rubber tapper and his family in the vicinity of Manaus (Amazonia).

54.
Three children playing with a water rat (Cotia, Pará).

55-61.
The birdlife of Amazonia and Pantanal is amazingly varied, often highly colorful. Parrots were included in the first cargoes shipped home by the Portuguese. According to a 1982 U.S. National Academy of Science report, a typical four-square-mile patch of Amazonian rain forest may contain 400 different birds and 125 kinds of mammal.

58

9

62

0

63

1

62, 63.
The Amazon and Pantanal have many creatures in common. The jaguar (Panthera onca), the largest of the cat family in the Americas, is heavier than its Old World cousin, the leopard or cheetah, but just as speedy and agile.

64.
The 350 varieties of fish found in Pantanal provide sustenance for many of its mammals, such as the otter (Lutra annectens).

65.
A lynx. In Pantanal wild animals — deer, ocelots, pumas, wild boar, anteaters, tapirs, the large capybara — live together with man and his domesticated animals in an unusual form of coexistence.

66.
Pantanal, the world's largest bird sanctuary, provides refuge for over 600 different species, from the six-foot tninin to a wide variety of parrots.

66

67.
The toucan, a bird of the Amazon. Wildlife in Pantanal is much like that of the Amazon, only more accessible than in the dense rain forests.

67

68.
Near Manaus (Amazonia) children
master a repertoire of tricks which
they perform with large water snakes.

69.
A fisherman coming home with his
catch, Ceará state, northeast Brazil.
Many kinds of shellfish, especially
lobster, are plentiful off the coast of
Ceará.

70, 71.
Amazonia's vast territory offers a unique experience for the nature lover. The oldest species of plant life on earth are to be found in the Amazon basin.

72.
Rescuing a monkey from a flood near Balbino (Amazonia). During tropical rains the Amazon may inundate an area 125 miles wide.

73.
A gold prospector's family (Cotin, Pará) during one of the brief visits they can make to the gold field.

of *Thea viridis* came from Macao in 1812, marking the beginning of the cultivation of tea in Brazil.

The famous Maracanã soccer stadium near the center of the city is the biggest in the world: it can accommodate 200,000 cheering fans. The bay of Rio de Janeiro is dominated by the 12,000-ton statue of Christ the Redeemer, arms raised in benediction, on Mount Corcovado ('Hunchback').

Copacabana, edged by a magnificent promenade, is the best known of the city's lovely beaches. Hundreds of youths play soccer on the sands of Copacabana, hoping that one day they, too, may achieve fame.

At the entrance to the bay rises a massive granite rock called Sugar Loaf Mountain, 1320 feet high, its precipitous slopes a challenge for climbers. Its summit was reached for the first time in 1817 by a thirty-nine-year-old Englishwoman, Henrietta Carstairs, who planted the British flag on the conquered peak. The next day Sergeant José Maria Gonçalves, considering this an affront to Portugal, undertook the arduous six-hour climb and replaced the British flag with the Portuguese. He was later discharged from the army for unknown reasons.

The first railroad from Rio de Janeiro to Petropolis, the summer residence of the Brazilian emperor, Pedro II, was built under the supervision of British engineer William Brag. The Emperor's Palace, a modest but elegant building reflecting the character of the emperor, is now the Imperial Museum, completely furnished with possessions formerly belonging to the Crown.

Minas Gerais, as the saying goes, has a heart of gold and breast of steel. The attractions of the region are the old colonial towns built during the gold rush in the eighteenth century and a number of spas and mountain resorts.

Among the treasures of the colonial towns are the collections of works by the world-renowned Brazilian sculptor, Antonio Francisco Lisboa (1734-1814), son of a Portuguese architect and an African slave, better known by the name of Aleijadinho, 'the little cripple'. An invalid, probably suffering from leprosy, in his later years he had to work in a kneeling, even lying position, his hammer and chisel tied to his arm. Perhaps his finest achievements are the powerful statues in the gardens and on the altar of the church of Bom Jesus de Matosinho in Congonhas do Campo. Much of his work is in Ouro Prêto, but other remarkable examples are to be seen in the towns of Sabará, São João del Rei and Mariana.

When a mulatto named Duarte Lopes, member of a prospecting expedition in Minas Gerais, discovered a nugget of pure gold in a mountain stream, fortune-hunters quickly flocked to the area. The next year, 1701, Mass was said for the first time, in a thatch-built chapel, in the place later to be called Vila Rica. In a few decades the small settlement had grown into a splendid city with fine buildings and churches raised by wealthy townspeople, providing employment for numerous artisans, contractors, painters, sculptors and wood carvers. The builders included Portuguese architect Manuel Francisco Lisboa, father of the future sculptor, Aleijadinho.

74.
An old man with a rooster at an
open-air market in Cachoeira, an
important commercial center in the
south of Bahia state.

Vila Rica, now Ouro Prêto, was granted city status in 1711, and became capital of the Minas Gerais captaincy in 1720. Situated in a valley and climbing rocky slopes, this one-time boom town with its splendid eighteenth-century buildings, fountains, thirteen churches, lovely gardens, and towers with enameled tiles has been proclaimed a national monument. The famous School of Mines has an outstanding minerology museum with precious stones.

Ouro Prêto abounds in Baroque carvings in wood and soapstone by Aleijadinho. The church of São Francisco de Assis and the façade of the church of Nossa Senhora de Carmo are also his work, as well as two pulpits in the church of São Francisco, a Baroque masterpiece combining beauty of architecture, expressive sculpture, and opulent interior decoration: gilded altars, statues, and paintings on the walls and ceiling by Manoel de Costa Athayde (1732-1827). The works of this eminent artist here and in the church of Santa Efigenia were painted with pigment made from iron ore and berries. The interior of Santa Efigenia is gilded with gold dust washed from the curly hair of African slaves upon leaving the mines.

On Independence Square stands a statue honoring a hero of the struggle for Brazilian independence, José Joaquim da Silva Xavier, better known as Tiradentes (Tooth-puller), leader of an unsuccessful revolt in 1789. As a souvenir of its past, every year on June 24 Ouro Prêto becomes for that day the capital of the federal state of Minas Gerais.

The city of Congonhas do Campo is dominated by a large church of pilgrimage, Bom Jesus de Matozinho, famous for twelve large statues of the prophets by Aleijadinho, one of the most outstanding art works of the period.

The church of São Francisco de Assis in São João del Rei, its outer and interior design by Aleijadinho, is another splendid monument of Brazilian Baroque, sumptuously adorned with gilded altars and other works of art. The visitor's eye is drawn to the French Baccarat chandelier, similar to one at Versailles.

Once the center of diamond mining, Diamantina has well-preserved colonial buildings, among them the house of Chica da Silva, an African slave who married a wealthy diamond prospector in the eighteenth century, becoming a popular heroine for the Brazilian blacks. The founder of Brasília, President Juscelino Kubitschek, was born in the town.

The south of Minas Gerais has several well-known mineral spas. One of these was visited by Princess Isabel, daughter of Emperor Pedro II, who was seeking a cure for barrenness. She subsequently gave birth to three sons.

Três Corações in southern Minas Gerais is the birthplace of Edson Arantes do Nascimento, better known as Pelé, Brazil's most famous soccer player.

The Center-west - A Future in Ranching

Three fifths of the central-western plateau comprise four federal states: Goiás, Mato Grosso, Mato Grosso do Sul and Tocantins, plus the Federal District of Brasília. This region occupying 22 percent of the national territory has a population of only ten million. The climate is tropical, semi-humid; the vegetation, a type of savannah grassland called *campo cerrado* growing about three feet high, with only the occasional tree.

The Araguaia River dividing the states of Goiás and Mato Grosso, navigable for some 990 miles, is known for its sandy banks and good fishing.

Half of Mato Grosso is covered by forests, and a large portion is under swamps. The most extensive area of flood plain, Pantanal, (about 38,400 square miles), lies between the cities of Cuiabá, Campo Grande in the state of Mato Grosso do Sul, and the Bolivian border. The largest bird sanctuary in the world, Pantanal shelters over six hundred different species: the six-foot tuiuiu stork, herons, ducks, quail, parrots, etc. Pantanal also has 350 species of fish, among them the giant pintado and voracious piranha; its animals include deer, ocelots, pumas, wild boar, anteaters, tapirs, the big amphibious capybara, and the most formidable of all, the often-photographed *jacarés*, or Brazilian alligator.

In some mysterious way the wilderness has brought its inhabitants together: in Pantanal man and his domesticated animals have found a *modus vivendi* with the wild creatures, which generally do not interfere with farm life. Most of the fauna of the region has therefore remained intact. During the rainy season, when a large part of the territory is inundated, the animals gather on several islands above the water, where ocelots and pumas can be seen lying peaceably alongside deer and capybara.

Immensely rich in fauna, Brazil has regrettably done little to protect its wildlife. Until recently 300 to 400 alligators were killed in Pantanal every month. From 1950 to 1965 about eight million alligators were hunted down in Amazonia.

Cuiabá, capital of Mato Grosso, stands at the geographical center of South America. The city was founded in 1719 when a Paulista expedition led by Pascoal Moreira Cabral and Miguel Sutil discovered gold here. Some 45 miles from Cuiabá is an unusual geological formation, the Diamond Plateau (Chapada Diamantina), about 3.5 billion years old, with many fossils of fish, indicating that Mato Grosso was once under the sea.

Mention of Mato Grosso immediately brings to mind huge ranches grazed by millions of cattle, the principle source of the state's wealth.

Goiânia, capital of the state of Goiás, is Brazil's second planned city, after Belo Horizonte. In half a century its population has grown from 800, mostly herders, to one million.

The Center-west region supports over 40 million head of cattle, though at the same time the large area under rice, manioc, beans, cotton and sugar cane is constantly expanding. If present trends continue, the region could become the world's leading meat producer. The huge estates (*fazendas*) with thousands of head of cattle, the opening up of new grazing land and the aerial sowing of grass seed make this development possible. Land is still measured, as at the beginning of colonization, in leagues (a league, the old land mile, is equal to 72,900 square feet). A tract of 250 to 500 acres is considered just a small fenced pasture here.

The central-western plateau is known as the land of the Indians, of gold (panned in the rivers), open-range ranches, canyons, explorers and hunters. In this century Mato Grosso has attracted many adventure-seekers from abroad: looking for wild Indians, exploring the jungles, studying wildlife, going on dangerous hunting expeditions, and searching for lost cities. In 1913-1914 Colonel Theodore Roosevelt, former president of the U.S.A., led an expedition to South America for the American Museum of Natural History. He was accompanied through the wilderness of Mato Grosso, traveling on foot and by canoe, by Brazilian general Cândido

Rondon, head of the Service for the Protection of the Indian, himself of Indian descent. After exploring the Duvida River, Colonel Roosevelt described his adventures in a book entitled *Through the Brazilian Wilderness*.

In Mato Grosso the first and perhaps only foreigner ever to kill a jaguar on foot and single-handed was a Russian, Sacha Siemel. Known as the Tiger Man, he had been taught by an Indian called Joaquim from the Guato tribe.

Colonel Percy Harrison Fawcett, a noted British explorer, made many expeditions to Mato Grosso seeking the lost cities which he believed to exist there. In April 1925 he set off with his son from Cuiabá on his last expedition, never to return. It is assumed that they were killed by Indians of the Kala-palo tribe on the Kuluena River.

The state of Tocantins in the valley of the Araguaia is called the 'Mesopotamia of Goiás' because of its fertility. This federal unit was separated from the state of Goiás in 1988. The region began to develop rapidly thanks to the construction of Brasília: moving the capital here boosted settlement and provided employment. It is also a major intersection for north-south communications linking Brasília with Belém, São Paulo and Rio de Janeiro.

The Northeast - Tradition and African Influence

The nine federal states of the region: Bahia, Sergipe, Alagoas, Pernambuco, Paraíba, Rio Grande do Norte, Ceará, Piauí and Maranhão, have a sense of unity which is based more on history than geography.

Of the five regions of Brazil the Northeast takes precedence in a historical framework. It was on this part of the coast that the first Portuguese navigators landed and made their discovery of Brazil. The first capital of the colony, Salvador, was established here in 1549. Its states, Pernambuco and Bahia, used to be the greatest producers of sugar for the world market.

The region, 18 percent of the national territory, is home to over 28 percent of Brazilians, including about half of the country's rural population.

The coastal belt, 60 to 125 miles wide, is under Atlantic cover (*zona do Mata*), an area with fertile soil, abundant vegetation, a humid climate and rain all year round. The second zone further inland (*zona do Agreste*) is a transitional zone, not so fertile, with less rain. The third zone, known as the *sertão*, is an arid region with poor soil, prone to natural disasters: long droughts and sudden floods. The problem of drought will require a long-term solution, using the São Francisco River to irrigate the vast complexes of arable land in the region.

Agricultural and livestock productivity remains low owing to the use of outdated farming methods. One of the main obstacles to progress is the structure of property ownership: the region is characterized by huge unproductive estates (*fazendas*) and debt-ridden smallholdings. Since the economy cannot absorb the growing labor force, there is considerable movement to the major urban centers and to regions offering better prospects for new settlements and farming.

There are few blacks living in the interior; the inhabitants are mainly of Portuguese-Indian descent. During rainy periods there is an abundance of food: goat's milk and cheese, sweet potatoes, beef, beans, but when winds from Africa parch the land in the interior, the consequences can be drastic. Waves of migrants move to the coast and southward until the first rains, when they return to their homes.

The chief exports are sugar, cotton and cacao. The eastern part of the region produces almost half of Brazil's sugar and cotton, while cacao is raised in southern Bahia. This region, particularly the state of Ceará, is known for its abundance of seafood, above all shellfish, the reason for the 'lobster war' with French fishermen during the Sixties.

In every important period in the history of Brazil the Northeast has played an active role: the long wars with the Indians, the struggle against foreign occupiers (French and Dutch), the suppression of revolts by African slaves, the fight for Brazilian independence. History and cultural tradition have helped shape a special feeling of unity, stronger here than in any other part of the country. These states now collaborate on a regional basis in many matters, particularly development.

This region, too, was caught up in the process of intensive urbanization. The capital cities of Salvador, Fortaleza and Recife now have over a million inhabitants each and continue to grow.

Salvador, capital of Bahia state, was the seat of colonial government for more than two centuries, down to 1763. It is the center of the tobacco industry, producing particularly fine, mild cigars, and the state's main port. A city of 135 churches and 27 museums, Salvador is built on two levels, the upper part (Centro) poised on cliffs and slopes rising some 250 feet above the sea. Sightseeing in the upper section takes the visitor back through the centuries. From Castro Alves Square one passes by the church of São Bento with its splendid seventeenth-century furnishings, the Geographical and Historical Institute, then the fort of São Pedro and the Castro Alves Theater. One should also walk along Oceanica Avenue, past the lush botanical gardens and climb Ondina for a view out to sea. The lower part of the city also has well-preserved buildings from the colonial period with heavy, carved wooden doors. Blessed with an ideal climate (a mean temperature of 78°F), spectacularly sited and crammed with masterpieces of Baroque architecture, it is no wonder Salvador ranks second only to Rio as a tourist mecca.

Both Salvador and Recife are renowned for their carnivals in which everybody takes part, wearing fanciful costumes, dancing and singing in the streets for four days. A colorful addition to the city are the black women of Bahia, in their traditional white costumes dating from the eighteenth century. They are generally street vendors hawking spicy snacks made of fish, vegetables and fruit.

African influences are strong in this one-time center of the slave trade. On the night of December 31 people head in groups for the shore to present gifts to the water goddess, Iemanjá, a ritual borrowed from African mythology. Another fascinating vestige is the *capoeira* dance, which evolved from the traditional foot-fighting brought by slaves from Angola. The dance is accompanied by music on drums and marimba, the beat getting faster and faster.

Candomblé, a copy of the *macumba* of Rio de Janeiro, is a local form of worship. Both *candomblé* and *macumba* are basically black African cults, the difference being that *candomblé* has kept closer to its African roots, while *macumba* has incorporated many Catholic and Indian elements.

One of the best ways to understand Salvador and Bahia is to read the works of the great Brazilian novelist, Jorge Amado, mostly set in southern Bahia, in the region of the cacao plantations where the author was born, and in Salvador or its surroundings.

At Recôncavo, 22 miles from the city, in the old Fregesia mill (1552) is the Wanderley Pinho Museum with documents and pictures illustrating three centuries of local life. The owner's home, Casa Grande, and the slave quarters (*senzala*) have been preserved intact. Recôncavo was a center of the sugar and tobacco industries in the sixteenth century.

From Ilheus in southern Bahia, near the mouth of the Cachoeira River, comes 65 percent of the cacao produced in Brazil. The town is the setting of the celebrated novel by Jorge Amado: *Gabriela, cravo e canela* (Gabriella, Cloves and Cinnamon).

Recife, like Salvador, has administrative buildings and houses dating from the colonial period, churches from the sixteenth, seventeenth and eighteenth centuries, and several museums. The best known of its many churches is the magnificent Golden Chapel (1697), built with Franciscan contributions for the prosperous families of Recife and Olinda who did not wish to mix with the blacks, mestizos and poor. The opulent interior is lavishly decorated with gold, hence its name. The Sugar Museum has models of colonial sugar mills, instruments used for torturing slaves, and a collection of old containers for sugar. In 1706 the first Brazilian printing press was founded in Recife, which also claims to have published Latin America's oldest daily newspaper (*Diario de Pernambuco*, 1825).

Olinda, founded in 1535 as the first capital of the province of Pernambuco, is another city famed for its many ornate churches and monasteries from the colonial period, filled with valuable paintings, sculpture, furniture, wood carvings. Well-preserved seventeenth-century public buildings and houses are embellished with latticed balconies, heavy doors and elaborate molding. The Museum of Sacred Art in the beautiful seventeenth-century Bishop's Palace has a remarkable collection of rare exhibits from the churches of Recife, Olinda, Igaraçu and Itamaraca. The old prison of the Inquisition now houses the Museum of Art of Pernambuco. There is also the old marketplace where slaves were sold, but no trace remains of the period.

In Igaraçu, 19 miles north of Recife on the road to João Pessoa, is the first church built in Brazil, dedicated to SS Cosmas and Damian. A large part of the city, founded in 1535, with many colonial houses and the first Masonic Lodge in Brazil, has been proclaimed a national monument.

Fortaleza, capital of the state of Ceará, is a handicrafts center (lace, embroidery, rope hammocks, clay figures).

The delightful climate, long, sandy beaches, unpolluted sea, the abundance of tropical fruit and seafood, and spicy local dishes have made the coastal belt of the Northeast increasingly attractive to tourists from Europe, especially in the wintertime when it is summer in Brazil.

Away from the coast, life in the Northeast is often harsh, making its inhabitants a very sturdy breed. Even in times of drought or flood, when they must leave their homes temporarily or permanently, these people never forget their love for their native land, convinced they will return. The challenge of life here has inspired the works of several Brazilian writers from this region: Gilberto Freyre, Jorge Amado, Euclides da Cunha, José de Acancar.

The North - Amazonia

The federal states of Amazonia, Pará, Acre, Rondônia, Amapá and Roraima, which make up the northern region, account for 42 percent of the national territory but only 5.6 percent of the country's total population. Its density in the state of Amazonia is no more than 1.6 inhabitants per square kilometer.
per square kilometer.

Most of the region is low-lying, the climate hot, above 77°F, with little annual variation. Humidity exceeds 80 percent. Rains are heavy during most of the year and cause considerable erosion.

The immense expanse of Amazonia abounds in many different kinds of exotic timber: rubber, oleaceous trees, trees producing various types of resin and medicinal substances. Its tropical hard and soft woods: jacaranda (rosewood), mahogany, etc., used for high-quality modern and period furniture, have long been a major export item. In consequence, there has been over-cutting and serious damage to the balance of nature.

The mineral wealth of the region has not yet been sufficiently explored. Prospecting suggests large reserves of oil, iron ore, gold, bauxite, manganese, zinc, etc. Today the Amazon basin is no longer the subject of romantic fantasies about hidden treasure. Instead, it boasts one of the greatest mineral deposits in Brazil — Carajás, in the federal state of Pará — already under exploitation. The Carajás reserves (66 percent FE content), estimated at over 18 billion tons, are the world's largest deposit of high-quality iron ore. At the present rate of production, for domestic use and export, the reserves will last another five hundred years. In Brazil it is hoped that Carajás may be only one of several such ore deposits in the unexplored Amazon.

The harmony of nature that reigns in Amazonia can rarely be found elsewhere on earth. According to botanists its rain forests are the oldest formations of plant life on earth, essentially unchanged since the Tertiary. Amazonia has almost a third of all species living in the world. The astonishing variety of its wildlife, a large part still unknown, is considered by some scientists a bounty even more precious than its mineral wealth. Six out of ten species live in tropical forests, and only 30 percent have been scientifically classified. On a single tree in the Amazon one can find 43 types of ant, the total number in the whole of the British Isles.

Today the principal danger, drawing ever closer, lies in the destruction of the planet's greatest genetic source, and without previous scientific investigation of its potential for the benefit of mankind. The pace of destruction of species living in Amazonia is estimated to be five hundred times faster than the laws of nature would account for.

Tropical jungles produce at least 25 percent of all pharmaceutical substances employed in modern medicine, from quinine, used for almost a century to wage a successful war against malaria, to therapeutic chemical substances for the treatment of cancer. Medicine suppressing high blood-pressure is found in the poison of the Amazonian jararaca snake, which acts on its victims by lowering their blood pressure to zero. The leaves of the jaborandi, growing only in the eastern part of Amazonia, yield an extract for eye drops treating glaucoma.

The Amazon is the longest river in Latin America, and the largest in the world in volume of water — seven times the volume of the Mississippi. It holds one fifth of all the fresh water on the earth's surface. More than two thirds of the length of this river and its basin are in Brazil, the rest in Peru, Bolivia, Ecuador, Columbia and Venezuela. Inhabiting some of its tributaries are electric eels and bloodthirsty piranha, attracted to their victims, including human beings, by the smell of blood. These tiny fish are capable of devouring an imprudent cow in only a few minutes, their sharp teeth tearing away the flesh like a saw, leaving only the bones.

The Amazon has the tasty tucunaré, the 'salmon of the Amazon', while the Araguaua River in Mato Grosso is known for the highly prized pirarucú, often weighing over 220 pounds. The Maué Indians use the dried tongues of this fish, hard as steel, to shred the dried berries of the guaraná, used to make a now popular beverage (guaraná) which they believed to be an elixir.

Amazonian fauna is exceptionally diverse. The jungles provide habitats for many kind of monkey, jaguars, pumas, tapirs, ocelots, deer, capybara, and in the waters of the Amazon, Brazilian alligators (*jacarés*) and many other amphibious creatures. The jungles are the denizen of innumerable kinds of snake, some of the world's biggest — the sucuri (the Amazonian anaconda) — and most venomous — the coral and urutu.

Amazonia has a wide variety of birds: eagles, hawks, many kinds of parrot, doves, pheasants, woodpeckers, toucans. Visitors to this region and certain other parts of Brazil admire the graceful acrobatics of the *beija flor*, a type of hummingbird. Originating in the Andes, on the border between Ecuador and Columbia, the hummingbird can now be found from Alaska to Patagonia, from sea level to the 16,000-foot heights of the Cordilleras, from the Pacific to the Atlantic. Brazil has myriads of these tiny birds, weighing only about half an ounce, which consume several times their weight in food every day.

Though, according to the original treaty, Amazonia should have belonged to Spain, in the sixteenth century Portuguese expeditions began to penetrate this territory. Pedro Teixeira crossed the entire region, reaching Quito in Ecuador. On the site of present-day Manaus, capital of the state of Amazonia, Francisco da Nota Falcao raised the fort of São José do Rio Negro in 1660.

The name Amazon, it is said, goes back to the sixteenth century when a Spanish explorer, Francisco de Orellana, was attacked by long-haired Indians on a part of the Amazon in Peru. Believing them to be Amazons, the legendary women warriors, he named the river after them.

In 1616 an expedition led by Francisco Caldeira Castelo Branco built a fort on the site of the present-day capital of the federal state of Pará, giving it the name Belém (Bethlehem) since the expedition had set out

76.
Guanabara Bay with the city of Rio de Janeiro. The Portuguese first mistook this magnificent natural harbor for a wide river estuary — hence the name January River. At the entrance to the bay rises the granite Sugar Loaf Mountain, 1280 feet high. ▶

77, 78, 79.
At any time of day, in any weather, Rio and its incomparable natural setting present a spectacle of breathtaking beauty. For once, man has not marred nature. ▶ ▶▶ ▶▶▶

75.
The statue of Christ the Redeemer, a landmark of Rio, dominates the bay from its perch on Mt. Corcovado (Hunchback). Weighing 12,000 tons and almost 100 feet tall, it was completed in 1931.

80.
Morro dois irmaos (Twin-headed
Peak) rising above Rio's Leblon
beach, one of the most popular in the
city.

81.
Fountains are a tradition in Brazilian
architecture, an attractive feature of
any urban setting, classical or
modern.

82

82.
Bathers on Rio's crowded beaches are part of the sensual image of this city, renowned for its beautiful women.

83.
Surfers on the beach of São Conrado, Leblon. Skillfully riding the waves, surfers are a popular attraction of the city beaches.

83

84

84.
View of Copacabana, one of the
world's most fashionable beaches,
from the Hotel Meridien. The boys
playing on the sands of Copacabana
may be future soccer stars.

85.
Ipanema beach, a picturesque parade
of beach boys and girls. Bronze
bodies and the bright colors of
swimsuits highlight this picture of
youth and beauty.

85

86.
Soaking up the sun on Ipanema
beach in Rio.

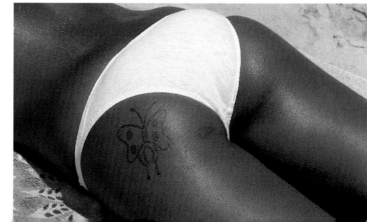

87.
An approaching storm. The ominous rain clouds are a warning to leave the beach in a hurry.

87

88.
Riders on a beach in Maranhão state in northeastern Brazil. The Bumba meu Boi festival on January 24 in São Luis, capital of Maranhão, features fantastic masks and bullfights.

88

89

89.
Rua da Quitanda in the downtown
shopping district of Rio, always
crowded at midday.

90.
A Rio streetcar popularly called
'Bondinho' (little streetcar), not far
from the center of town, near
Flamengo. Initially the streetcars
were operated by a British company
and, to attract passengers, each fare
served as a lottery ticket.

91.
Samba dancers. When the carnival
ends, soloists and ensembles perform
the best songs and dances at the
Plataforma, a famous Rio restaurant.

92

92.
Street entertainers are a familiar sight
in Rio.

93.
Rio's Maracanã, the world's biggest
soccer stadium and the pride of
Brazil. ▶

94.
A family from a favela. The migration from countryside to town in search of work or better pay has steadily worsened housing conditions in the biggest Brazilian cities.

97.
A fisherman from Ceará, his lined face etched with age and the hardships of his life. ▶

94

95.
A boy from a favela. Rio de Janeiro and other conurbations are trying to provide better education and medical care for the children of these shanty towns.

96.
Rocinha, the largest of several dozen favelas in Rio, is home to 300,000 of the city's poor.

on Christmas Day. On the Rio Pará, 80 miles upstream from the Atlantic, it was an excellent place to protect navigation and launch expeditions into the Amazon, but also to block the penetration of French, British, and Dutch pirates. Nineteenth-century Belém grew into a fine, European-style city thanks to the opening of the river to international navigation and the rubber boom.

Traveling in the Amazon, French naturalist Charles Marie la Condamine became acquainted with the primitive use of wild rubber and after his return submitted a report to the French Academy of Science. The French adopted the Indian name *caoutchouc* for the substance, while the Portuguese called it *borracha*.

After the discovery of the multiple uses of rubber, from vulcanization to waterproofing, its price on the world market rose steadily. By 1910 rubber production was worth 62.5 million dollars, 20 percent of total Brazilian exports, but by 1930 only one percent (according to 1910 prices).

Plantation owners in the region, 'rubber barons', soon made fortunes. Fantastically rich, but often with little education, the new millionaires of the Amazon wanted to embellish their capital cities of Manaus and Belém, transforming them into tropical versions of Paris. Manaus was the second city in Brazil to introduce electric light and the first in South America to have streetcars. Deep in the interior, 900 miles from the mouth of the Amazon, this city with regularly traced streets, impressive public buildings and splendid mansions, took the greatest pride in its fabulous opera house, the Amazon Theater, a symbol of the town's prosperity. Caruso, who performed at its opening, was the first of many world-famous artists to appear there. Conceived as a replica of the Paris Opera, its marble was transported from Italy, murals were painted by De Angelis and Caprenesi, and crystal chandeliers imported from Bohemia. But the heyday of opera on the Amazon is now long past: this theater which can seat 1000 is now used only once a month.

The rubber barons and their families, striving to compete with the European aristocracy, maintained a luxurious life style, following the latest fashions and purchasing their wardrobes in Paris. The buildings of the time are a reminder of this age of conspicious consumption. Even the big Customs House was built in Moorish style, with blocks of granite transported from Scotland, while the covered market was modeled after a French railway station. Manaus, second largest city in the region, was then (and has remained) a major port for exports not only from western Amazonia but also from Peru, Bolivia and Columbia.

The Indians also played their part in the rubber boom. The Portuguese colonists had long ago seen the Indians tapping the rubber trees (*Hevea brasiliensis*) and curing the latex over smoky wood fires. Drawing on the Indian experience, the European Brazilians improved the technology of rubber production. Two of the Tupi tribes made a special contribution to the culture of the region. The Cambeba taught the settlers about making rubber and the Maué tribe, about guaraná, a fruit now used in a refreshing beverage of this name and as a powder promising health and longevity.

In 1876, an Englishman, Henry Wieham, secretly carried to Great Britain several thousand seeds from the rubber tree, which he had labeled as orchids, and presented them to Queen Victoria. The seeds were planted first at Kew Gardens in London, where they thrived, and were then taken to the colony of Malaya. The operation was a huge success. By 1913 the production of Malayan rubber had outstripped that of Brazil:

47,000 tons against 39,000. Brazilian domination on the world rubber market now passed to British hands. The rubber boom, however, had brought more than transitory riches to Amazonia: it had encouraged significant immigration to the region, primarily from the Northeast.

Like the British with the rubber plant seeds, the Portuguese made off with the coffee bean. In 1727, on a trip to Cayenne in French Guiana to settle a border dispute, Francisco de Mello Palheta, an officer from Maranhão, won the affections of the wife of the governor of this French colony. According to this romantic version, the governor's wife put a few coffee beans into his cup as a parting gift. After returning to Brazil, he planted them, but not just as a souvenir of the beloved lady. The climate in Pará having proved unsuitable for coffee, in 1770 beans were sown on plantations in Bahia, and from there carried to the state of Rio de Janeiro. Coffee-raising then spread to Paraíba, São Paulo, Minas Gerais and Paraná. This was the beginning of a new economic cycle — following sugar and gold — the 'cycle of green gold'.

From 1840 onward coffee became a vital component of the economic progress and culture of Brazil. The path of coffee from Europe to Brazil was not uneventful, In 1665, when the first seedlings were brought from Turkey to Italy, arguments arose over whether a beverage of Muslim origin could be drunk by Christians. To the delight of coffee-lovers who, historians relate, included the head of the Catholic Church himself, Pope Clement IX approved the drinking of coffee by Catholics as well. Other great lovers of coffee in Europe were Rousseau, Voltaire, Richelieu and Diderot.

As the Portuguese and Spanish settlers in Amazonia mixed with Indian women, their offspring gradually became assimilated. This accounts for the special Indian cultural contribution in the North. Indian legends and art, ways of hunting, fishing and raising crops, household utensils, folk medicine, food and spices — all this is part of the Indian cultural heritage adopted by Brazilian society, especially in the North.

Three centuries of colonization, limited primarily to the river banks, did not result in large-scale settlement or exploration of Amazonia. Real exploration began only after the Second World War. It took a radar-based geological mapping program to uncover the secrets of the mineral wealth buried in the Amazon jungle.

Amazonia is rapidly changing. The 3,000-mile east-west trans-Amazon highway now links up with the north-south artery (Belém-Brasília). Mining basins and oil fields, industrial centers, power stations and highways have spurred settlement and employment, particularly of poor people from the Northeast.

The trip by boat from Belém to Manuas is an unforgettable experience. Halfway between the two capitals, at Santarém, the yellow water of the Amazon mingles with the greenish water of its tributary the Tapajós. Near Manaus is the five-mile-wide confluence of the Solimões, actually the Amazon, and the Rio Negro. At the confluence one can distinguish the bluish-black Rio Negro from the brownish-yellow water of the Solimões, the two rivers flowing one beside the other for several miles without mixing. This is explained by differences in the flora which give the water their color and in the weight of the water because of its mineral content and temperature. Only after four miles do the waters gradually mix, continuing together as the Amazon.

One of the symbols of the Amazon basin is the *Victoria regia*, a giant water lily, flowering in February-March. Its floating oval leaf can reach a diameter of six feet and support a weight of 150 pounds.

Belém, the capital of the federal state of Pará, is the metropolis of the whole region. Its cathedral, founded in 1719, is among the largest in Brazil. Like Manaus, Belém also has a theater, though less sumptuous, a combination of Classicism and Art Nouveau. In the era of the rubber boom, the box of the state governor was furnished with French chairs and Venetian lamps, and the interior of the theater with chandeliers made of Bohemian crystal.

Between Belém and Manus is Santarém, and 25 miles further, Belterra, where in 1927 Henry Ford established a rubber plantation and built a whole new town with small houses and a big hospital, staffed by Americans. Though the rubber plantation experiment was a failure, it demonstrated that people could live and work in Amazonia and still retain their health, a factor of importance for the future settlement of the region.

Pôrto Velho is the capital of the federal state of Rondônia, which is the focus of agricultural experiments and settlement projects. A good part of the land is reserved for Indians, but since 1980, the area covered by virgin forest has fallen from 97 to 80 percent.

Brasília - Capital of Hope

The idea of building a new capital in the central plateau dates from 1750, when map-maker Francisco Tossi Columbiana suggested more or less the present site. In 1832 José Bonifácio de Andrada e Silva made a similar proposal to the Constituent Assembly of Brazil. According to his scheme, the new capital, the seat of the Court or Regent, would be built in a healthy, fertile part of the interior. Having the seat of government in the center of the country would protect it from attack, roads to the new capital could promote internal trade, and its location would attract settlers to this sparsely populated part of the country. He also suggested a name for the capital — Brasília.

The first Constitution of the Republic (1891) endorsed the construction of a new capital, but work did not begin in earnest until 1956. President Juscelino Kubitschek inaugurated Brasília as the capital and the Federal District in 1960.

The city was designed by a distinguished urban-planner, Lúcio Costa, its most beautiful buildings were the work of the world-famous Brazilian architect, Oscar Niemeyer, and the landscaping was directed by Roberto Burle Marx. The city plan fits, roughly speaking, into the outlines of an airplane. The residential and business quarters are located in the 'wings', while the 'fuselage' has the government buildings, military and cultural institutions, banks, hotels and recreation centers. In the 'cockpit' is the Praça dos Três Poderes with the buildings of the National Congress (the House of Deputies and Senate), the palace of the President of the Reublic and Supreme Court. The Piazza of Three Powers is said to be the real heart of the Brazilian state, an architectural symbol of the legislative, executive and judicial powers. Situated along the 'tail' are the railway station, shopping center and industrial area. Most of the diplomatic missions are in the Avenida das Naçõ es. Near the city is the man-made lake of Paranoá, created to give moisture to the air during the dry season.

Brasília, lying in the middle of the arid, undeveloped, *sertão*, at an altitude of 3800 feet above sea level, has a temperate climate. The federal administration was understandably reluctant to move from Rio de Janeiro to Brasília, 580 miles inland, and the diplomatic corps took their time about it. Energetic measures and deadlines were required, first to transfer all the government agencies, and then the embassies. For a long time many federal officials kept their families in Rio de Janeiro and São Paulo, traveling home for the weekend.

Today, three decades after its birth, the prophetic words of French minister André Malraux have been fully borne out: impressed by the city plan, Malraux called Brasília the 'capital of hope'. Its democratic atmosphere owes much to the influx of people from all over the country, making the capital the most Brazilian of cities.

Brasília encountered for the first time is a memorable experience. A marvel of modern urban-planning and architectural design, this 'city of the twenty-first century' indeed offers a hopeful vision of the future.

A short distance from Brasília is a natural phenomenon called the Aguas Emendadas. Two streams rising in the same place flow in opposite directions, eventually forming Brazil's two largest river systems: the Amazon in the north and the Rio la Plata in the south. On the territory of the Federal District is the watershed dividing the largest Brazilian river basins: the Amazon, Paraná-La Plata and São Francisco. In the same direction, a few miles north of the town of Formosa, are the waterfalls of Itiquira, the highest (525 ft.) in Brazil, an awe-inspiring sight that seems to epitomize all the wild beauty and untamed power of nature.

'Portuguese Landing in Brazil': engraving, a contemporary artist's impression of this event (1500).

From Colony to Republic

Outpost of Empire

The colonization of such a vast territory as Brazil was a very lengthy process, beginning with the establishment of small trading posts (*feitorias*) along the coast, for the purpose of claiming territory and asserting Portuguese sovereignty.

In 1534-1536 a system of hereditary captaincies was established, but little headway was made, either in colonization or in the discovery of precious metals and gems.

When the first governor general arrived in 1549, he was accompanied by functionaries experienced in colonial administration, soldiers to secure the coastal area, Jesuit and Franciscan missionaries to convert the natives to Christianity. They were soon followed by the first groups of African slaves.

Sugar production quickly developed as the chief activity, while cattle were brought in from the Azores to start livestock farming. The sugar-cane plantations, however, required a great deal of labor, for which the native Indians were found unsuitable. On the other hand, the Portuguese settlers from Madeira, the Azores and the mother country were few in number. The problem could be solved only by bringing in African slaves.

The early Portuguese settlers were not accompanied by their families, which naturally led to unions with Indian women. Their offspring, the mestizos, were to become a significant demographic factor in the settlement and development of the colony. With the ships of the second governor general, in 1553, came a group of Portuguese orphan girls, dispatched by the Regent Catherine to make a life with the settlers. This marked the start of regular transports of female orphans from the mother country.

The Role of the Church

In the Portuguese colonies the Roman Catholic Church had immense wealth at its disposal. The primary source was the tithes which every Christian regularly contributed for the support of the Church. By papal decision this money, believed to be the largest source of revenue during the colonial period, was collected by the Portuguese Crown. With these funds the Crown aided the organization of the Catholic Church in the colony, built churches, supported monastic orders. The money also helped finance the conquest of new territories. The second source was the concessions granted by the Holy See for the expansion of Portugal on the basis of a papal bull, *Da Santa Cruzada*, which remained in effect even after Brazil acquired independence. The contributions were voluntary, but were collected by the Church through the existing system of taxation. Part of these huge resources was used to maintain fleets and military forces in Africa, Asia and Brazil.

The first members of a monastic order to be sent to Brazil were Franciscans, followed by Jesuits, and later Benedictines and Carmelites. Despite the great prestige they enjoyed in Portugal, the Benedictines did not set up monasteries in Brazil. It was Jesuit missionaries who requested the Portuguese Crown to establish the first see, but they soon came into sharp conflict with the first bishop, Pero Fernandes Sardinha, who arrived in Brazil in 1552. In his view, conversion to Christianity meant that the natives should be Europeanized. He was scandalized by the conduct of Jesuit missionaries who had adopted some of the Indian customs, for example, nudity. Nor did he approve of the Jesuits' using the Tupi language to say Mass or the incorporation of Indian songs, dances and musical instruments into religious services.

The Jesuit missionaries and Portuguese colonists later petitioned the Crown to found a university in Brazil, a request that was not granted. The Overseas Council, which administered the colony, regarded university studies in the mother country as one of the strongest ties binding the dependent territory to the metropolis, and for this reason gave priority to the granting of scholarships for the famous Portuguese university at Coimbra.

After the expulsion of the Jesuits from Brazil in the mid-eighteenth century, the Franciscans developed their monasteries as centers of learning and the Catholic faith. In 1776 the monastery of Santo Antônio in the center of Rio de Janeiro drew up a statute detailing a public course of philosophy and theology with eight subjects and thirteen professors. The first aspirations to national autonomy in the ecclesiastical sphere were expressed in these monasteries, where fierce rivalry between locally-born priests and those from Portugal came to the fore.

In the opinion of Brazilian historians, the indigenous clergy were instrumental in creating a Brazilian national consciousness and a feeling of attachment to Brazil.

Era of Expansion

The expulsion of the French was decisive in consolidating Portuguese rule over the whole Northeast and over Rio de Janeiro in the Southeast. This was followed by struggles with the Dutch in the Northeast.

The annexation of southern Brazil meant fighting the Spanish and their colonies in Uruguay, Argentina and Paraguay. To secure expansion into the Amazon basin it was necessary to drive out the Spanish, French and others. There are particularly moving stories about the incorporation of Amazonia into Brazil, as the Carmelites, Capucines and, especially, the Jesuits fought to protect the peaceful Indians from the cruel expeditions of the Portuguese settlers.

Cattle-raising, especially in the Northeast, opened up a vast, virtually unpopulated area in the interior of the country. As the cattle moved, dependent on climatic conditions and pastures, the territory of the colony was steadily enlarged. Thus, huge areas were conquered by a handful of people. The search for gold and precious stones and the expansion of livestock farming from the Northeast led settlers westward to the central parts, which were then incorporated into Brazil.

Disappointed at first in their search for gold and gems, the Portuguese, like the Spanish in Mexico and Peru, created a myth of an enchanted land in the center of the continent, Eldorado, with hills of emeralds and diamonds. For centuries the legend attracted explorers and adventurers.

Seeking gold and new territory, groups organized like army companies, the so-called *bandeiras*, set off into the interior, mainly from the São Paulo region. During an expedition the leader, or captain, had both military and civil powers. Indians joined them, voluntarily or forcibly. Some of these units were perpetually on the move, pushing northward for several years on end. In 1693 Antônio Rodriguez de Arzao found large quantities of gold in the present state of Minas Gerais, sparking off the great gold rush that attracted thousands of Portuguese from all classes, from the poorest to the nobility. These expeditions into the interior, especially to the west, finally made Brazil the largest country of Latin America.

The first geographical survey of the whole territory of Brazil, *Corografia brasilica*, including all the provinces, was published by Aires de Casal in 1817.

A Nation in the Making

The expansion of the colony was especially encouraged by the energetic colonists from Portugal, but also by the descendants of settlers who had formed unions with Indian and, later, African women.

Aware of the need to increase the sparse population of this huge colonial posession, the Marquis of Pombal drafted laws that encouraged the Portuguese to marry Indian women. The state granted them arable land, tools, seed grain, cattle, exemption from taxes on their produce and from military service. The children of these marriages, called *caboclo*, had the same rights as members of the families of colonial settlers. Though the state encouraged marriages with Indian women, mixing with African slaves was officially banned and thought shameful. It all depended, however, on the local legislator: some Portuguese settlers ignored the official ban and the children of these marriages, mulattoes, were considered legitimate.

Adrien Balbi estimated the population of Brazil in 1810 at 3,617,900, of which 843,000 were whites, 259,400 Indians, 426,000 freemen of mixed descent, 202,000 slaves of mixed descent, 159,500 black freemen and 1,728,000 black slaves. In 1818 the population was put at 4,222,000.

Settlement during three centuries of colonial rule did not progress as hoped. Though the number of Portuguese colonists and their descendants was disproportionate to the size of the territory of Brazil, the settlement of foreign immigrants was not permitted until the middle of the first half of the nineteenth century.

Colonial policy, moreover, did not promote the integration into Brazilian society of the Amerindians, or the African slaves and freemen. The efforts of prominent Portuguese and Brazilians in the nineteenth century, and of certain Brazilians in the twentieth, did not essentially change the position and prospects of the indigenous population, their number already drastically reduced by enslavement, extermination as their lands were seized for expansion into the interior, and decimation by diseases transmitted by the Portuguese. Between 1743 and 1749 in the villages created and maintained for the Indians by Catholic missionaries, in Amazonia alone, 40,000 Indians died of smallpox. Intermarriage between Portuguese and Indian women virtually ceased after the arrival of other European immigrants, thus interrupting the process of racial integration.

In the second half of the nineteenth century hundreds of thousands of Europeans settled in Brazil: Germans, Italians, Portuguese, Poles, Ukrainians, Hungarians, Swiss and others. In the first half of the twentieth century came the Japanese, Spanish, Russians, Yugoslavs and others. The opening of Brazilian harbors to ships from friendly nations and the free settlement of European immigrants accelerated demographic growth and economically activated the most important parts of Brazilian territory. Rio de Janeiro, the capital, served as a catalyst in the integration and unification of the country, guiding the policy of the colony in preparation for emancipation.

The Paths of Independence

More than three centuries of total Portuguese domination in the colony did not permit any degree of autonomy. All the authority was concentrated in Lisbon, in the hands of the Overseas Council and the king. The viceroys, first in Salvador and then in Rio de Janeiro, did not have wide powers. When the Portuguese Court, fleeing Napoleon's troops, took refuge in Rio de Janeiro, the city acquired a new role, replacing Lisbon in political affairs. Thus began a process of 'governing Brazil', which was the main consequence of the presence of John VI. This is judged to be one of the principle reasons why Portuguese Latin America in the fateful hour of independence did not split up into several states, as did Spanish Latin America.

Though a distant colony, Brazil could not remain unaffected by progressive trends and turbulent events in the United States, France and Europe at large. In the final years of Portuguese colonial rule, popular discontent mounted. Four serious plots were registered. The first was the 'miners' conspiracy' in 1789 in Minas Gerais, officially known as the *inconfidência mineíra*, actually a national revolutionary movement for Brazilian independence. It all began in the city of Vila Rica, today Ouro Prêto, whose population during the gold rush had climbed in just a few years to 100,000, making it bigger than the capital Salvador, and four times the size of São Paulo.

Around the mid-eighteenth century in gold-rich Minas Gerais an educated élite began to emerge, susceptible to ideas from Europe and North

98.
A gaucho in Rio Grande do Sul returning at dusk with his flock of sheep. The mixing of Portuguese settlers with native Indians produced this typical representative of the region.

99.
The pampas. Sunset on the range in Rio Grande do Sul, the great meat producing region of Brazil. ▶

100.
A herd of cattle driven home at sundown in Rio Grande do Sul. To the multi-faceted picture of Brazil the gaucho has added a pastoral way of life, a picturesque costume, a style of cooking, songs and dances. ▶ ▶

101.
Marajó island at the mouth of the Amazon, the largest river island in the world (area: 15,444 sq. miles), is another region where cattle can be raised. ▶ ▶ ▶

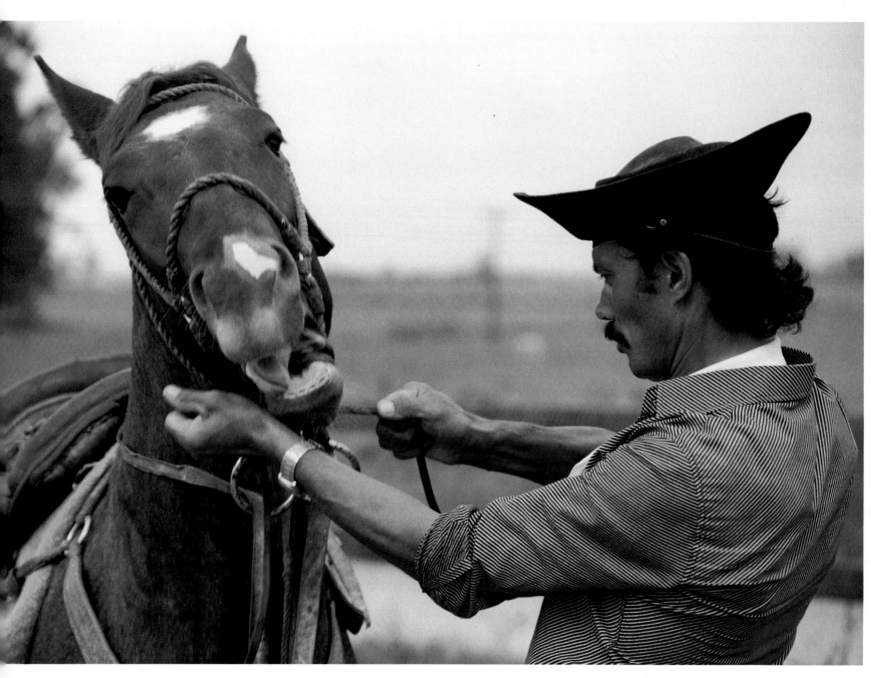

102

102.
The gaucho and his horse are
inseparable, and Rio Grande do Sul
is the land of the gauchos, the
'cowboys' of Brazil.

103.
A herd of cattle. The gauchos
developed a distinctive way of life as
ranchers or frontier guards on the
southern border. A gaucho speciality:
churrasco, charcoal-grilled beef.

103

104.
A flock of sheep at sunset in Rio
Grande do Sul, an area opened up for
crop and livestock farming in the
present century. ▶

105.
Gauchos on horseback, Rio Grande
do Sul. Initially nomads, today
farmers and ranchers, they have not
abandoned their elegant style of dress
though some innovations can be seen.

105

106.
Two leather-clad riders in
Pernambuco. Roaming the arid
northeastern plains, the vaqueiro, the
northern counterpart of the gaucho,
wears leather to protect himself from
thorny scrub and cacti.

107.
In Pantanal, as in other ranching
regions, horses are highly valued and
carefully groomed.

108.
Returning from pasture in Pantanal.
Cattle-raising is concentrated in
central and western Brazil. If current
trends continue, the region could
become one of the largest meat
producers in the world.

109.
A gaucho in traditional dress, Rio
Grande do Sul: a wide-brimmed
brown hat, baggy trousers, wide
leather belt, a lasso for roping cattle
and a special knife for cutting meat. ▶

America. Many had become politically active while studying at European universities. A student at Montepellier, José Joaquim da Maia, even met Thomas Jefferson, U.S. president from 1801 to 1809. The guiding spirit of this revolutionary movement was a second lieutenant in the cavalry, Joaquim José da Silva Xavier, known as Tiradentes ('Tooth-puller'). One of the plotters betrayed the plan of rebellion, and Tiradentes was arrested in Rio de Janeiro. Having accepted full responsibility at his trial, he was publicly hanged and quartered in Rio de Janeiro on April 21, 1792, as a deterrent to all future conspirators. Tiradentes became a national hero, symbol and forerunner of Brazilian independence, still some thirty years in the future.

This and other plots of rebellion were clear signals, which the mother country could not, or would not, understand, that the independence of the colony was now on the cards. The movement towards statehood, in evidence throughout Latin America, was accelerated in Brazil by its economic, cultural and national development. Over 3,000 Brazilians completed their studies at the Portuguese university in Coimbra. The Overseas Council was vigorously opposed to offering higher education outside the mother country, aiming to secure a loyal colonial élite closely bound to the metropolis. Yet this same intellectual élite, educated in Portugal and other European countries, was the vanguard in the fight for independence.

Statehood in Sight

When Napoleon invaded Portugal, Britains's ally, in 1807, he surely had no idea he was inaugurating a new era in the history of Brazil. But so it turned out.

Prince Regent John, together with the royal family, several thousand functionaries and half the national treasury, fled the country under the protection of the British fleet, sailing first to Salvador in Bahia, and then to Rio de Janeiro. Upon his arrival in Salvador, one of his first acts was to open up Brazilian harbors to friendly nations (*Carta Régia*, January 29, 1818), the first important step towards economic independence for the colony. The ending of earlier trade restrictions, i.e. monopolies held by Portugal, likewise led to the rapid growth of commerce. British goods flooded the Brazilian market and maintained their supremacy until the late nineteenth century, when Britain lost its leading industrial and trading position to the U.S.A.

Reforms that followed fundamentally changed the position of the colony. Brazil, in fact, is the only instance in history of a colony becoming the seat of government of its mother country. In 1815 its status was enhanced by the proclamation of the United Kingdom of Portugal, Brazil and the Algarves. Brazil was given the same institutions of administration and the judiciary as Portugal. After the death in 1816 of Queen Maria I, who had been insane for years, the prince regent became King John VI, and for the first time the sovereign received heads of diplomatic missions in Rio de Janeiro.

The coequal status of the mother country and the colony was not welcomed in Portugal, especially in powerful trading circles. In 1820, under threat of a military revolt at home, King John VI was forced, after thirteen years, to return to Lisbon, leaving behind his son Dom Pedro as regent.

The Portuguese Cortes (Parliament), striving to preserve the unity of the empire, abrogated Brazil's autonomous status in 1821. Relations between Brazil and the mother country rapidly deteriorated and the call for independence grew ever louder.

The regent refused to obey the order to return to Lisbon, relying on the support of the Brazilian population. At the same time, he appointed to the new government the distinguished Brazilian, José Bonifácio de Andrada e Silva, known as the 'Patriarch of Independence'. On September 7, 1822, in São Paulo, Regent Pedro solemnly proclaimed the independence of Brazil and its secession from Portugal. His declaration ("I shall remain" and "Independence or death") followed several futile attempts to maintain contact with Portugal. The youthful regent was crowned Pedro I, Emperor of Brazil, in Rio de Janeiro on December 1, 1822.

Resistance to the proclamation of independence existed in Brazil as well, especially in provinces with a strong concentration of Portuguese troops (Bahia, Maranhão, Amazonia in the north, and Rio Grande do Sul in the south). Lord Dundonald, a British naval officer who had entered Brazilian service, played an important role in obliging the Portuguese garrisons to leave Brazil.

The Imperial Age

The early years of the new empire were fraught with political crises. Experience in self-government was lacking and Emperor Pedro I tended toward absolutist rule. The Portuguese aristocracy was replaced by Brazilian landholders who opposed any change in the political and economic system, while big business, the middle class and intellectuals favored radical social changes and a republican form of government.

Recurring clashes between the emperor and the Constituent Assembly further widened the gulf between Pedro I and the people. The first Constitution, 1824, granting the emperor absolute power, provoked serious rebellion in the northeastern provinces (Pernambuco and Pará). The revolts were put down by force, but the discontent remained. After an unsuccessful war with Argentina (1827) and the proclamation of the independence of Uruguay (1828), Pedro I was compelled to abdicate in favour of his minor son, Pedro de Alcantara, in 1831.

During the period of the regency, the turbulent 1830s, a number of rebellions broke out as the power of the absolutist monarchy weakened and demands increased for greater provincial autonomy. At the same time, republicanism gained ground. The regency was partially successful in dealing with the crisis and preserving the unity of the empire, but demands for federalism, though postponed, persevered.

In 1840, in order to preserve the existing system, the young emperor, though only fourteen, was declared of age, so ending the rule of the regents. The following day a liberal government was formed.

The reign of Pedro II, lasting almost half a century, is considered the most prosperous in Brazilian history, while the emperor himself is held in respect as a simple, modest, democratic monarch. Parliament was active; the state apparatus functioned well. The economy, especially foreign trade, developed rapidly, boosted by investment of foreign capital, particularly British, and large-scale immigration from Europe.

As in the colonial period, political power remained in the hands of the landowners, the social and economic élite of Brazil. During the nineteenth century agriculture was the main source of wealth (coffee, sugar, rubber, tobacco, cacao), especially after gold-mining declined.

In Brazil the struggle to abolish slavery was a long one. The issue had been raised in the early nineteenth century, largely by members of the educated classes. The leader of the abolition movement was a well-known attorney and writer, Joaquim Nabuco, who insisted on an immediate and complete end to slavery, which 'poisons the life of the Brazilian nation'. The provinces of Ceará and Amazonia abolished slavery in 1844, and some ten years later the importation of slaves finally ceased. In 1870, when Brazil was virtually the only western country still using slave labor, a law was passed emancipating all future offspring of African slaves.

The question of slavery was a constant source of conflict between the Court, which favored gradual abolition, and the plantation owners, throughout the period of the monarchy, and was finally instrumental in its fall. The complete abolition of slavery, without compensation to the slave-owners, was decreed on May 13, 1888, by the regent Princess Isabel in the emperor's absence. About 700,000 slaves were freed. But the Crown did not long survive this humanitarian act. On November 15, 1889, the republic was proclaimed. Marshal Manuel Deodoro da Fonseca assumed the duties of prime minister in the interim government, and the emperor and his family left Brazil.

The overthrow of Pedro II is still a subject that intrigues many Brazilian and Portuguese historians in view of the prosperity of Brazil during his reign and the sovereign's great personal popularity. Certainly the creation of the republic did not come as a result of popular discontent and social protest. But the monarchy lost the support of the Church and conservative forces, particularly the plantation owners. This, coupled with the growth of republican sentiment, made the collapse of the empire inevitable, and Pedro II abdicated, dying in Paris in 1891. Also contributing to the appeal of a republic was the fact that Pedro II lacked a male heir, and the throne would be inherited by his daughter Isabel, married to a French aristocrat.

The First Republic

The first two presidents, Marshals Manuel Deodoro da Fonseca and Floriano Peixoto, were military autocrats, yet during their incumbencies several progressive measures were implemented: the separation of Church and State, the institution of civil marriage, and the first Constitution of the Republic (1891), modeled on that of the United States. All the provinces of Brazil were united as a federation named the United States of Brazil (*Estados Unidos do Brasil*). A bicameral congress was set up consisting of the Senate and the House of Deputies. Executive powers were in the hands of the President of the Republic, assisted by a vice-president and a presidential cabinet. The federal states during the First Republic likewise had presidents. As the states were entitled to levy export duty, the two wealthiest, São Paulo and Minas Gerais, wielded greater influence than the others in national politics: the office of president was usually held in turn by statesmen from São Paulo and Minas Gerais. Even today politicians from the state and city of São Paulo have better chances in elections for leading posts in the Federation.

The military presidents were followed by three civilian presidents, a period marked by rapid growth. President Manuel Ferraz de Campos Salles (1890-1902) is remembered for having rescued Brazil from financial chaos after the overthrow of the monarchy. President Francisco de Paula Rodriguez Alves (1902-1906) is judged the most capable civilian president of Brazil. During their terms of office these two were served by a very able foreign affairs minister, Baron do Rio Branco (1902-1912), who successfully resolved some of Brazil's most sensitive border questions.

During the incumbency of President Wenceslau Brás, (1914-1918), Brazil broke off relations with Germany after the torpedoing of several Brazilian ships and declared war on October 26, 1917. He sent part of the Brazilian fleet to European waters and medical units and pilots to the Western front. The country's greatest contribution to the Allies, particularly to the U.S.A., was in supplying food and raw materials, which also permitted Brazil to stabilize its economy.

Brazil participated in the Versailles Peace Conference in 1919 and was given a temporary seat on the Council of the League of Nations.

The transformation from empire to republic did not generate many significant political changes, but the federal states and municipalities were granted wider powers. Large-scale immigration from the Mediterranean countries before and after the First World War spurred the growth of the coffee industry, especially in the state of São Paulo.

Postwar development was interrupted by the Great Depression (1929-1933), accompanied by a drop in the price of coffee, fluctuating prices for raw materials and, inevitably, internal unrest and strife.

In 1930 the opposition, with the aid of the army, carried out a coup and installed a three-man military junta. The leader of the insurrection, Getúlio Dornelles Vargas, governor of the state of Rio Grande do Sul, assumed the duties of provisional president. This marked the end of the First Republic and beginning of a very important phase of the country's history: Brazil changed more after 1930 than during the entire preceding period. After 1930 the states no longer had presidents but governors.

The Second Republic

Vargas' first fifteen years of rule were characterized by greater involvement of the State in national life and a series of rebellions of various kinds. Vargas was an authoritarian president whose program was to integrate the interests of all the federal states and pursue a unified national policy.

While he was in power, Brazil declared war on Germany and its allies (August 22, 1942) after the sinking of five Brazilian merchant ships by German submarines, resulting in the loss of 607 lives. Brazil was the only Latin American country whose troops participated in the Second World War. Brazilian units fought courageously on the Allied front in Italy in 1944 and 1945. The Brazilian Expeditionary Corps (20,000 men) under General João Baptista Mascarenhas de Morais was with the American 5th Army under the command of General Mark Clark.

Vargas' fifteen-year rule was marked by economic and social progress, but also rising discontent. Fearing another Vargas coup, the army removed him from office in 1945.

Postwar Progress

The end of the Second World War ushered in a period of industrialization and rapid economic growth. The people, borne on a wave of anti-fascist, democratic aspirations, ventured onto the political stage.

One of the first measures of the new president, Enrico Gaspar Dutra (1946-1951), was to abrogate the Vargas Constitution of 1937 and promulgate a new, more liberal one in 1946.

The estate-owning oligarchy hoped to regain its former ascendancy, while the bourgeoisie sought greater privileges. Foreign capital was given greater security, the powers of the central government were reduced, the conservative section of the middle class gained influence.

During Vargas' second incumbency (1951-1954), citizens' constitutional rights were respected, the labor unions were supported; the state had a bigger say in the economy and formed monopolistic state-owned companies. In 1954 came one of the greatest crises in modern Brazilian history, as wave after wave of unrest and strikes swept the country, provoked by corruption, inflation and poor living conditions. Unable to resolve the crisis and faced by powerful, behind-the-scenes pressure to resign, President Vargas committed suicide.

The next elected president, Juscelino Kubitschek de Oliveira (1956-1961), is remembered for his interest in settling the interior of the country and building a new capital, Brasília, far from the coast. In foreign affairs Kubitschek advocated a policy of multilateral cooperation between North and Latin America in the field of economic development, advising the United States of the grave economic problems of Latin America. His program Operation Pan-America was accepted by all the Latin American states and anticipated the Alliance for Progress.

The winner of the next presidential election, Jânio da Silva Quadros, resigned after little more than half a year because of conservative opposition, and was succeeded by his vice-president, João Belchior Marques Goulart.

President Goulart (1961-1964) attempted radical reforms of the socio-economic system, most notably agrarian reform and nationalization of the oil refineries. Strong opposition, primarily from landowners and the army, led to his overthrow by a military coup on April 1, 1964.

For the next twenty-one years, until the victory of the presidential candidate of the democratic opposition, Tancredo de Almeida Neves, on March 15, 1985, Brazil was governed by a military regime.

Illustration from the 'Livro dos
Armadas', a sixteenth-century
Portuguese account of the voyages of
Vasco da Gama and his captains.

National Goals

It has been said that Brazil was a nation before it became an independent country. Its national aims took shape already during the colonial period, becoming more clearly defined after independence. Regardless of differences of emphasis, these aims were basically: unity, territorial integrity, national integration, democracy, economic development, cultural identity and an independent foreign policy.

Unit and Territorial Integrity

Unlike the developed autochthonous civilizations of the Andes, which were more resistant to Spanish colonization, the primitive cultures of the various Indian tribes scattered across Brazilian territory posed no serious obstacles to the unification of the Portuguese colony.

From the very outset the fight to defend the coutry's territorial integrity against French, Dutch and Spanish incursions was experienced by the Portuguese settlers, and in some degree by the Indians and Africans, as a struggle to preserve national unity. According to historians, the Dutch invasion (1630-1654) drew together masters and slaves, whites, Indians and blacks, Portuguese and Brazilians, inhabitants of different captaincies. It fostered a consciousness of the unity of the Brazilian nation.

The Portuguese Crown, confronted by the daunting task of governing this huge and distant possession, in 1572 divided the colony into two parts, appointing one governor general in Salvador (Bahia) and another in Rio de Janeiro. Realizing very quickly the problems that might arise from the fragmentation of the colony in view of the constant threat of foreign intervention, the Crown abolished this dualism in 1577, and made no further attempt to partition Brazil.

It should be mentioned that in 1789 the Brazilian national hero Tiradentes demanded freedom for Portuguese America, but not its fragmentation: he and his associates supported the preservation of Brazilian unity. It is likely that his views were influenced by the example of the North American fight for independence. The revolt in Pernambuco in 1817, when a short-lived republic was proclaimed, was the first real threat to internal unity.

The demands for a federation, for wide powers for the provinces, later federal states, did not compromise the country's unity, for they merely sought greater autonomy. The main emphasis in the Proclamation of the Republic in 1889 was on federation, decentralization, regional political and administrative autonomy, but within the framework of Brazilian national sovereignty.

During the later nineteenth and early twentieth centuries, by means of treaties with neighboring countries all border issues were resolved, so that today there are no frontiers under dispute.

National Integration

From the very start the concept of integration had two aspects: unification of all parts of the vast Brazilian territory — while respecting regional economic and cultural differences — and social integration of the different racial, religious and social groups. This long-term policy was pursued from the beginning of colonization — the settlement of the coastal belt.

The discovery of precious metals and gems triggered off large-scale penetration into the interior and its gradual settlement.

Several great river systems helped link up the Brazilian interior. The indigenous population and Portuguese settlers traveled along tributaries of the São Francisco — from the northeast to the southeast and central western part, along tributaries of the Amazon — from the coast to the interior of Amazonia, and along tributaries of the Rio la Plata — from the south to the central-west and north.

Ranching in the Northeast and South and the constant movements of the herds also opened up vast areas, particularly the central parts of Brazil.

Coffee and rubber likewise played their part in the process of expansion and integration. Initially the coffee plantations spread from Rio de Janeiro to São Paulo, then to Minas Gerais and Espirito Santo. Rubber, essential for British and North American industry in the second half of the nineteenth century, spurred further settlement and integration of the Amazon basin. The extraction of latex from the rubber tree (*Hevea brasiliensis* or *Hevea amazonica*), which grew naturally in the Amazonian jungle, attracted hundreds of thousands of people. The majority came from the Northeast (Ceará), particularly during periods of drought.

The building of telegraph lines and land survey stations, railways and roads, followed by the gradual linking up of major cities by air lines, all speeded up national integration. Since the Thirties, radio has been an important factor in this process, and since the Sixties, television.

110.
The cathedral, Igreja da Će, in the center of Sao Păulo. Belying its Gothic appearance, it was built early in the twentieth century.

111

111.
The Jockey Club in São Paulo.
Together with the Brazilian Jockey
Club in Rio de Janeiro, it plays the
leading role in promoting equestrian
sports, above all, horse racing.

112

112.
São Paulo is the biggest industrial
and financial center in Brazil and
Latin America. Here different races,
religions and nationalities live
together in harmony, a true example
of social integration.

113

113.
Soldiers on parade. São Paulo
celebrates the Constitutional
Revolution mounted in the city on
July 9, 1932, against President
Vargas, who governed without
benefit of a constitution. Though the
rising was put down, a constitution
was promulgated in 1934. Only São
Paulo commemorates this event.

116.
Skyscapers pierce the clouds. São Paulo ranks among the world's biggest cities. From 580,000 in 1920, its population has soared to around 10 million in the metropolitan area. ▶

117.
Ouro Prêto, formerly Vila Rica. Its wealthy inhabitants raised elaborate monuments to the dead, such as these statues at a cemetery on the outskirts of the city. ▶ ▶

114.
Veterans leading the parade on Revolution Day in São Paulo.

115.
One of the many fountains that grace and refresh the city of São Paulo.

114

118

118.
'Head of Christ', a dramatically expressive sculpture by Antonio Francisco Lisboa, always known as Aleijadinho, the greatest artist and architect of the Brazilian colonial period. One of his finest works is the church of the Bom Jesus in Matozinho (Minas Gerais).

119

119.
'The Last Supper', considered by
many to be Aleijadinho's great
masterpiece. Christ's grave
countenance is in striking contrast
with the gestures and expressions of
the Apostles.

120

120.
The Orthodox church in São Paulo,
an impressive edifice with a
sumptuous interior, built between the
two world wars.

121.
The momumental exterior of the Orthodox church is echoed in its interior design. In a city populated by 98 different nationalities of many different religious persuasions, the Orthodox community includes Greeks, Russians, Yugoslavs, Bulgarians, etc.

121

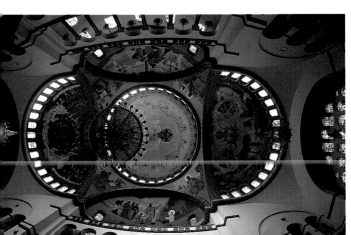

122.
Detail of the ceiling of the Orthodox church in São Paulo. Both exterior and interior reflect the influence of Byzantine architecture and wall-painting.

122

123.
The monastery church of São
Francisco in Salvador (Bahia), famed
for its gold-covered interior and fine
statues carved in wood.

123

124.
The church of Nosso Senhor do
Bomfim in Salvador (Bahia), best
known for its festival of the 'washing
of the Bomfim', is another example of
Brazil's exuberant Baroque
architecture.

125.
São Francisco in Salvador (Bahia) is
the richest church of the many in this
lovely city, which as the seat of the
colonial governor was the first capital
of Brazil.

126.
Statue of Pomba Gira, Manaus
(Amazonia).

127.
The convent of our Lady of the
Angels in Penelo (Alagôas), a typical
example of Franciscan architecture in
Brazil.

128.
The church of São Francisco de
Assisi, Ouro Prêto (Minas Gerais),
with fine Baroque carvings in wood
and soapstone by the celebrated
Aleijadinho, who was also the
architect. When it was completed in
1794, the Baroque style was already
outmoded in Europe but still
flourishing in Latin America. ▶

The integration of the Indians began soon after the arrival of the first Portuguese settlers, who mixed with Indian women from the Tupi-Guarani tribes. The natives of the coastal region, large groups of Tupi, spoke a common language, were more culturally advanced and assimilated more easily. Their assistance was considerable in driving out the French and Dutch.

The wild Tapuias, Aimorés and Goitacases, further inland, who did not speak the Tupi language, stubbornly resisted assimilation, eventually suffering the tragic fate of total annihilation.

Despite the ban in 1565 on procuring slaves from the Tupinambás tribes, two centuries were to pass before a law abolishing Indian slavery was finally enacted in 1775.

For a time the Portuguese-Tupi dialect (*lingua geral*) spoken in São Paulo and Amazonia threatened the unity of the Portuguese language, prompting measures to stem this development. Indian influence is strongly felt in local toponyms and names for plants and animals.

Since independence Brazil has tried to resolve the problems of the Indians with varying degrees of success. In 1910 the Service for the Protection of the Indian (*Seviço de Proteção au Índio* - SPI) was set up. In 1968 the National Foundation for the Indian (*Fundação National do Índio* - FUNAI) was established, merging the National Council for the Protection of the Indian and the Indian Park at Xingu. Five years later the Indian Statute (*Estatuto do Índio*) was voted. Prominent Brazilian anthropologists, Indian experts, missionaries and others have accused the FUNAI of improper application of the Indian Statute.

The election of the chief of the Xavante tribe, Mario Juruna, as a deputy to the Federal Assembly from Rio de Janeiro encouraged the Indian community to take a more active approach to the defense of their rights and interests.

Though Portuguese settlers, without their families, were by law free to mix with Indian women, this was not the case with African women. Many, however, disregarded this ban. The extent of racial intermingling is reflected in the Brazilian vocabulary. Mestizos is the general name for persons of mixed blood. The children of a white-Indian union are called *coboclo* or *cariboca*. The children of white and black parents are known as mulattoes, while the offspring of an Indian-black union are called *cafuzo* or *caboré*.

Religions have become integrated as well as races, especially in Bahia and Rio de Janeiro, where the Catholicism of the white colonists merged with the beliefs of the African slaves in cults known as *candomblé, macumba* and *umbanda*. The divinities of the Sudanese Yoruba tribe came to be identified with certain Catholic saints, for example, Oxóssi with St. George, the Iboji twins with SS Cosmas and Damian.

Since independence the various kinds of racial prejudice formerly prevalent among the wealthiest classes, the clergy, army and civil servants have gradually diminished.

From the early years of its statehood Brazil pursued a policy of encouraging and controlling immigration. Between 1822 and 1975, some 5,600,000 immigrants came to Brazil: 31.5 percent were Portuguese, 28.6 percent Italian, 12.9 percent Spanish, 5.3 percent German, and 4.4 percent were Japanese and other nationalities. Their gradual integration with the Brazilian population was effected by measures aimed at breaking down geographic and social isolation, checking the creation of national enclaves within the country, encouraging the introduction of Brazilian families into existing immigrant communities, and ensuring the integration of schools and the entire school system. As a result of this policy the Germans and Japanese, who initially isolated themselves in their own communities, have also merged into Brazilian society, as have numerous groups of Arabs and Jews, who live together today without any problems, regardless of the situation in the Near East.

Immigration has not changed the character of Brazilian life but enriched it. With all its diversity and contrasts, modern Brazil is much more homogeneous, linguistically and culturally, than other large countries. This integration has had a decisive role in fostering a strong feeling of belonging to Brazil, of patriotism, among all its citizens.

Foreign Policy

Events in the early years of statehood soon revealed the weakness of the Brazilian giant. The former Spanish colonies in Latin America were mostly hostile, and Brazil was defeated by Argentina in a war that resulted in the loss of its southern province (now Uruguay). Certain great powers, including Great Britain and France, pressed for economic concessions with extraterritorial rights and for the payment of unwarranted compensation. Brazil resisted such demands and pressure, striving to preserve the territorial *status quo* and the country's independence.

As a counterweight to the efforts of the new Latin American states, formerly Spanish colonies, to gang up against it, Brazil sought closer ties with the United States, in order to avoid isolation on the American continent. This relationship was seen as a long-term guarantee of Brazilian integrity, independence and security.

Brazil's foreign policy, based on national interests and the maintenance of a stable, realistic position, has aimed to strike a balance between political, economic and military cooperation with the United States, Europe and Japan, on the one hand, and Latin American integration and solidarity with Africa on the other. It has opposed the formation of rival subregional groups in Latin America, but supports cooperation on a bilateral basis and among all the states collectively. Brazil is fully aware of its regional economic, political and strategic interests in the Amazon and La Plata basins.

Democracy

The liberation movements in the colony were inspired by liberal ideas on national independence and democracy current in the late eighteenth century.

The Provisional Revolutionary Government of Pernambuco, established after the revolt in this province in 1817, proclaimed a republic, guaranteed the rights of the individual, freedom of the press and opinion, freedom of worship — all basic liberal principles. The Provisional Government, which existed almost two and a half months, issued a document on the struggle for democratic institutions in Brazil, stating that sovereignty emanates from the people and prescribing a tripartite division of powers (legislative, executive and judicial).

Though essentially autocratic, the constitution of the Brazilian Empire (1824) was democratic with respect to the civil and political rights of Brazilian citizens, but black slavery was maintained. In 1834 the decentralization of imperial political institutions gave the provinces greater autonomy.

During the early years of the First Republic the regime manifested dictatorial and militarist tendencies; it was only with the first civilian president (1894) that democracy was introduced. Brazil then experienced alternating periods of democracy and authoritarianism, the army playing a major role in such reversals. On March 15, 1985, once again a parliamentary democracy was established, after twenty-one years of military rule.

Economic Development

The colonial economy developed in cycles, in response to the needs of Portugal and European markets. Portugal's trading monopoly on brazilwood was highly lucrative, and by the middle of the sixteenth century Brazil was producing more sugar than the Spanish part of Latin America. In the seventeenth century alone, exports of Brazilian sugar earned 200 million pounds sterling for the Portuguese Crown.

Besides sugar, Brazilian tobacco also dominated the world market, exports bringing in 12 million pounds sterling during the colonial period. Tobacco had been used by the Indians in religious ceremonies, and the Portuguese took up the habit. calling it 'holy grass' (*erva santa*).

From the cattle which had been introduced by the Portuguese in the first half of the sixteenth century, the colony first exported only hides, and then salt beef. In the early eighteenth century Brazil had about 1,500,000 head of cattle, and at the time independence was proclaimed, about five million. During the colonial period Brazil exported hides worth 15 million pounds sterling.

This was followed by a period of economic growth known as the 'gold cycle'. In the early sixteenth century Europe's gold reserves amounted to an estimated 50 million pounds sterling. Between 1500 and 1800, 300 million pounds' worth of gold poured into Europe from America, 200 million coming from Brazil. Most of this ended up in London, financing the Industrial Revolution in Britain.

The decline in mining coincided with the beginning of the 'coffee cycle'. In 1830 Brazil exported 400,000 sacks of coffee (one sack = 60 kg.), in 1840 over a million, in 1860 two million, in 1880 four million. The prosperity of the empire depended largely on slave labor on the coffee plantations. The republic likewise relied heavily on earnings from coffee, but produced by foreign immigrants, primarily Italians. Coffee exports (for example, 17 million sacks in 1900) provided the financial basis for the industrialization of Brazil, especially the state of São Paulo.

The first major drive for industrialization came during the First World War, when it was necessary to replace imported industrial goods. During the period from 1933 to 1937 Brazilian industrial production rose 50 percent. The Second World War also boosted Brazilian industry. With the country's immense resources of raw materials, its possibilities for economic growth would seem virtually unlimited.

Matriz Sto. Antonio
Tiradentes - 64,

Renée Lefèvre

Religion

Catholicism

Almost ninety percent of Brazilians officially declare themselves to be Roman Catholic, making this the largest Catholic country in the world.

The discovery and colonization of Brazil were accomplished jointly by the Portuguese state and the Catholic Church. Papal bulls, issued in 1455 and 1515, served as legal foundations for the king of Portugal and his heirs to control the Church in the colonies. One of the main aims of colonization was to convert the indigenous natives to Christianity, if necessary by force, "the cross and the sword acting together".

The Jesuits, six of whom arrived with the first governor general, Tomé de Sousa, in 1549, played the principle role in spreading Catholicism among the Indians, though many other orders, notably the Benedictines and Franciscans, were active in the colony. To protect the converted Indians from being taken as slaves and to integrate them into Brazilian society, the Jesuits settled them in villages (missions), many deep in the interior. Though baptised, the Indians were sometimes reluctant to abandon the practice of polygamy and cannibalism.

The Jesuits also pioneered education, founding the first school in 1550 in Bahia. To this and other Catholic schools orphans were sent from Lisbon to be trained for the priesthood. Until the nineteenth century, church schools and monasteries were the only providers of formal education for young Brazilians, who continued their studies in Portugal at the University of Coimbra.

The first Catholic school for girls was founded in 1667 in Salvador, Bahia. It was attended by girls from aristocratic and wealthy families, accompanied to school by black slaves, who remained in the service of their mistress even if the latter should enter a convent.

Though the missionaries were inspired by the noblest aims, the possibilities of earning a fortune in the colony later attracted unworthy priests from Portugal, who became owners of vast estates worked by Indians and African slaves. Enrichment likewise led to decadence among the Catholic hierarchy in the colony.

It was not long before the activities of the Inquisition in Portugal were felt in Brazil. The Court of Inquisition (Holy Office) in Lisbon deported primarily new Christians (converts from Judaism), suspected of still practicing the Jewish faith. The colony's population was thus augmented by several hundred Jews, mostly people whose property had been confiscated, one part always being assigned to the inquisitor.

The Church was also zealous in converting African slaves. After baptism they enjoyed a minimum of rights, for a Christian name entitled them to a residence permit, marriage, but no improvement in social position.

The number of priests in Brazil steadily increased. During the eighteenth century problems arose with priests coming from Portugal because of their privileged position among believers and in the Catholic schools and monasteries. On the other hand, native-born priests held increasingly independent views, opposing the official policy of the Portuguese state and Church.

Eventually the Jesuits became too powerful. Apart from running most of the educational institutions, they had great influence among the ruling classes and at the Portuguese Court as confessors of the royal family. Long resented by the richer colonists, the Jesuit missions were accused of inciting an armed revolt of the Guarani tribe against Spanish and Portuguese military units so as to retain the territory of Sacramento in southern Brazil as a semi-autonomous entity beyond the control of the Portuguese government. In 1759, taking advantage of a nearly successful attempt on the life of the Portuguese king, Joseph I, in 1758, his prime minister, the Marquis of Pombal, drafted a law expelling the Jesuits from all territories under Portuguese rule and confiscating all Jesuit property. In Brazil 25 residences of the Society of Jesus, 36 Indian missions, and 17 religious schools offering free tuition were closed. After this, the Church entered a long period of crisis, especially in the field of education.

The mid-nineteenth century was a time of radical change in the Catholic Church in Brazil. Its bishops sought to reform the colonial or 'traditional' form of Catholicism and secure its conformity with the universal doctrine propounded by the Holy See. This actually meant Europeanizing the Catholic faith in Brazil, restoring the prestige and power of Rome, and tightening up the Church's organization. The saints traditionally venerated during the colonial period were officially set aside, a ban which was impossible to enforce in practice, and more stress was laid on religious observances, including regular attendence at Mass. 'Traditional' Catholicism was a product of the shared life of Portuguese, Indians, Africans and mestizos in Brazil and, as such, adapted to Brazilian conditions. Its practices were liberal: beside the official liturgy, there were popular celebrations, and independent black Catholic fraternities which introduced African songs and dances into the forms of worship.

When the reorganized religious schools did not comply with the new scheme, seminarists were sent to study in Rome and France. Most of these religious schools were run by the Lazarists (members of the order of St. Vincent de Paul), and in São Paulo by French Capuchins.

In 1890 the Church was separated from the state, a move reflecting the religious tolerance characteristic of modern Brazil. The number of Brazilian priests rose, but also those from abroad. In 1974 one third of the Catholic priests in Brazil were foreign (Belgian, French, Portuguese, Italian, etc.). Today in Brazil beside the official Catholic Church there is also a popular Catholic Church supported by the lower and some of the higher ranks of the clergy.

Protestantism

The first three German Lutherans came to Brazil in the middle of the sixteenth century. In 1553 one of them, Hans Staden, published in Germany a book describing a land of savages, the Indian Tupinambás tribe, in whose captivity he had spent several months.

In 1555 a French expedition commanded by Nicholas Durand de Villegaignon arrived in Brazil with the intention of founding the colony of 'France-Antarctique' as a place of refuge for French Huguenots fleeing religious persecution. They settled on unoccupied territory which subsequently became the site of Rio de Janeiro. With the support of John Calvin, the Church in Geneva sent another group of 300 persons who, on March 10, 1557, held the first Protestant service in Brazil, led by their pastor Pierre Richier. But only ten years later the garrison was forced to surrender and withdraw from Brazil, together with the Calvinists and Huguenots.

After the Dutch occupation of Pernambuco in 1630, ministers of the Dutch Reformed Church endeavored to spread Protestantism among the Portuguese, African slaves and Indian tribes, but their evangelical activity was cut short by the military defeat and withdrawal of the Dutch in 1654.

The first Protestants in Brazil to receive official permission to practice their religion were German scholars belonging to the Lutheran Church and English technicians of the Anglican faith (1808 and 1810). The liberal views of Emperor Pedro II (1840-1889) made it possible for Protestantism to spread despite opposition from the Catholic Church. He believed that the future of Brazil depended on European immigrants, taking as his example the settlement of the United States. With the settlers came Protestant missionaries, British, German and others, who began penetrating into the interior.

The arrival of Protestant missionaries from the United States led to increased evangelical activity throughout Brazil, the building of churches, founding of religious schools and social activities. However, the Protestantism of the European newcomers did not gain widespread influence, because these groups, especially the German settlers, kept apart, and conducted their services in their own languages. Nevertheless, Protestantism gradually gained favor among the burgeoning Brazilian middle class, thanks to their liberal education and their special interest in progressive movements in North American society.

The Lutherans played the most prominent role in establishing Protestantism in Brazil. The first group began their activities in Nova Friburgo (state of Rio de Janeiro) in 1824. The Evangelist Lutheran Church of Brazil, of North American origin, was founded in 1900, at which date, according to official figures, the majority of the 143,743 Protestants (one percent of the Brazilian population) were Lutherans.

In the course of the nineteenth century, Brazilian Churches were founded in turn by the Congregationalists, Presbyterians, Methodists, Baptists and Anglicans.

Following the arrival of Pentecostal missionaries in 1910, the expansion of the Pentecostal Church was rapid: in 1930 10 percent of all Protestants in Brazil, in 1958 over 50 percent. According to official statistics for 1980, out of a total of 4,022,343 Protestants, 3,863,503 belonged to this Church.

Judaism

Cabral's expedition to India, which set sail from Lisbon in 1500, included several Jews experienced in navigation. It is believed that the physician Mestre João, who drew one of the maps of the discovered land (Brazil) sent to the Portuguese king, Manuel I, and the interpreter Gaspar da Gama, were of Jewish descent.

The Jews were among the first to realize and exploit the opportunities offered by this new territory. As early as 1502 a group of Jewish merchants in Lisbon, led by a recent Christian convert from Judaism, Fernando de Noronha, approached the king with a proposition for exploration of the colony and establishment of a chartered company at their own expense for developing trade. The charter, signed in 1503, was initially for three years but was renewed with certain modifications until 1515. The trade referred to was mainly the export of brazilwood, known then as 'Jewish wood' (*Madeira judaica*). Historians surmise that beside commercial interests Fernando de Noronha wanted to facilitate the exodus of Portuguese Jews, who made up the majority in his expedition. According to the charter, every year a fleet of six ships was to be sent to the colony for exploration, exploitation of the seaboard along a stretch of 300 leagues, and setting up fortified trading posts.

Whereas Christian colonists from Portugal were more inclined to settle in India, Portuguese Jews were drawn to Brazil. According to historians they proved able colonizers. They had experience of the sugar industry on the islands of Madeira and São Tomé, from which they brought the sugar cane to Brazil, and established good relations with the Indians, learning their customs and languages. By the end of the sixteenth century they owned about 200 sugar mills in the colony.

The Jewish community in Brazil in the mid-sixteenth century was numerous thanks to a steady flow of immigrants and natural growth; it was able to resist assimilation and enjoyed freedom of worship. But its position began to deteriorate after the ban on the immigration of converted Jews from Portugal to Brazil in 1567, and grew worse at the end of the century when representatives of the Portuguese Inquisition appeared on the scene. Alarmed, the Jews began to move from northeast to southern Brazil, expecially to the region of São Paulo, then the most liberal part of the colony. Instead of Brazil, Portuguese Jews started settling in western Europe, particularly the Netherlands, which allowed greater religious freedom.

The founding in 1630 of a Dutch colony in Pernambuco, the rich sugar-growing region in the northeast, was viewed as a fresh opportunity by the Jews, who soon made their mark in the sugar industry there.

129.
Carnival time in Recife. Young and old, rich and poor, forget their cares in this pre-Lenten festival celebrated in many Brazilian cities. At Recife, a small car leads the procession with the figure of a lion or elephant, followed by the carnival king and queen, with girls of Bahia in embroidered white dresses dancing on either side.

130, 131, 132.
The Rio carnival, one of the world's greatest spectacles, fuses Portuguese colonial tradition with elements of African culture. This feast of rhythm, color and glittering costumes takes a whole year to prepare. During its brief span, everyone is a friend and all inhibitions are cast aside. ▶ ▶ ▶

133.

The main event at Rio's carnival is the procession of samba schools at the Sambódromo (capacity 60,000). Each samba school in Rio represents part of the city and selects its own melody, theme, matching color scheme and costumes.

134.

134.
The Rio carnival climaxes with the samba contest. Victory brings great prestige and popularity, reward for long months of practice.

135, 136.
It is hard to stand out amid all the
bewildering color, movement and
razzle-dazzle of the carnival, but
everyone makes an effort. Enormous
ingenuity, imagination and labor is
put into the making of costumes, like
this elaborate confection of feathers.

139

137.
Every samba school has its star performer, generally a poor mulatto girl from one of the favelas. After practicing all year long, for a day or two she can forget the realities of her everyday life.

138, 139.
Rio's carnival has been called 'a folk festival with a modicum of clothing and an abundance of joy'. Thousands of dancers from the favelas surrender body and soul to the rhythm of the music. Given the warm February weather and the energy they expend, a modicum of clothing is all they need.

140.
During the carnival the lovely
mulatto girl, celebrated in many
works by Brazil's most distinguished
poets, composers and artists, is a
symbol of beauty and racial
democracy.

141.
The carnival in Recife (Pernambuco).
All their worries temporarily
forgotten, some spend a whole year's
savings on these festivities.

142.
African music has been present in
Brazil since the early colonial days
and the arrival of the first black
slaves.

142

143.
During the festivities, girls from the
favelas deck themselves out in
'diamonds' and finery they can
otherwise only dream of.

144

144.
One of the great attractions of the
Rio and other carnivals is the endless
inventiveness of the costumes. These
dancers could be Portuguese grandees
or pirates of the Spanish Main.

145

145.
A free interpretation of an Indian theme in a recreation of the Amazon jungle.

146.
At carnival time in Rio the tune and lyrics of every new samba are earnestly discussed. The music, like the festivities, is an inextricable mixture of races and cultures.

147.
At the carnival in Recife, a festival of youth and beauty, extravagance and imagination.

148.
Young revelers, overcome by fatigue at the Recife carnival, sleeping in the street after hours of dancing. ▶

149.
Fantastic masks are a feature of the Recife carnival. Disguised by mask or costume, the participants are freed of their normal constraints and can enjoy themselves to the full. ▶▶

Those who settled in the New Netherlands were mostly refugees from Portugal, Spain and France. In time they virtually controled economic life in this Dutch colony. The main street of Recife was known as the Street of the Jews (*rua dos Judeus*) and its waterfront as the Quay of the Jews (*cais dos Judeus*). The Jewish community in the city, numbering over 1500 persons, was larger than that of Amsterdam.

Towards the end of Dutch rule, about half of the Jewish colony left Pernambuco and returned to Holland. When the Portuguese recaptured the territory in 1654, most of the remainder emigrated to the Caribbean (Guyana and the Antilles - Martinique, Guadeloupe, Barbados, Jamaica, Santo Domingo) where they started to raise sugar. Some believe that it was thanks to these Jewish refugees from Brazil that Central America and the Caribbean came to dominate the sugar trade, once exclusively in the hands of Brazil.

The intensified persecution of Jews in Portugal, especially after 1683, increased the number of 'new Christians' immigrating to Brazil. The first half of the eighteenth century is known as the 'black period' in the history of the Brazilian Jews, who by this time, through trade and the exploitation of gold and diamonds, had become the wealthiest group in the colony. Persecution of Jews in Portugal by the Inquisition, which was then at its peak, spread to Brazil, where sentencing the Jews was the easiest way to confiscate their large estates.

After the abolition of the Inquisition in Portugal in 1759, the Jewish community in Brazil revived and prospered as before. Religious freedom was officially decreed in 1810. Soon after, the first group of Sephardim arrived in Amazonia, where the first synagogue, Shaar ha-Shamayim (Gates of Heaven), was founded in Belém in 1828. Towards the end of the century Jewish immigrants began to come from Greece, Turkey, Lebanon, Palestine, Poland and, especially, Russia.

Afro-Brazilian Cults

The first African slaves to reach Brazil, in the 1530s, were mostly from the Bantu peoples of Angola and the Congo, a smaller number from Mozambique and Madagascar. Later they were shipped from the Ivory Coast, Ghana, Togo, Benin, Nigeria, Guinea, Gabon, Guinea-Bissau. With them they brought numerous, very distinct cultures (languages, customs, beliefs, tales, legends, food, music, dances, costumes and especially religions), which in time were modified or disappeared. Exposed to different influences, the African forms of worship began to lose, in varying degrees, some of their original characteristics.

Despite strong Portuguese repression in the early period of colonization, the blacks managed to maintain their traditions and rituals through a superficial form of syncretism. In the nineteenth century numerous dispensations facilitated the preservation of African culture in Brazil.

This survival of African cultural values, however, should be attributed rather to a lack of interest on the part of the Portuguese slave-owners and the Catholic clergy in anything more than superficial conversion of the slaves to Christianity, than to their strong resistance to European cultural values. Condemned to a life of slavery in Brazil — after a brutal rupture of contact with family, village, tribe in their homeland — many blacks agreed to accept the sacraments and participate in Catholic ceremonies without ever forsaking their ancient beliefs and forms of worship.

As the Africans in Brazil became familiar with the beliefs of the Indians, they adopted some of them, and also the Indians' way of preserving their culture and beliefs. Under pressure from official Catholicism, they found a solution in linking African gods, the Orixás, with certain Catholic saints.

The first region where black slaves were brought was Bahia. Here people venerated the largest number of Orixás, deities derived from the Jeje-nago of Portuguese Guinea (today Guinea-Bissau). These form the basis of the *candomblé* cult, considered the purest and closest to its African roots. Bahia is still today the largest center of *candomblé*, which seems to be growing into the most widespread and popular cult in Brazil. Although North American and Brazilian slaves originated from the same regions in Africa, these gods were almost completely forgotten by the American blacks as a result of the influence of the Protestant faith, which forbade their worship, and in any case discouraged the veneration of saints.

The slaves who came to Rio de Janeiro were from the Bantu tribes of Angola. Here the *umbanda* cult, formerly known as *macumba*, emerged as an offshoot of *candomblé*. While the latter spread from Bahia to Pernambuco, Maranhão and Rio Grande do Sul, *macumba* and *umbanda* were carried from Rio to São Paulo and to some extent to Minas Gerais. These African forms of worship are also practiced in other countries of Latin America.

The word *candomblé*, recorded for the first time in 1828, during a revolt of black slaves in Cabula, Salvador (Bahia), now has several meanings: a place of worship, the sect itself, and its rituals. For most of its followers *candomblé* is a continuation of the traditions and beliefs of their ancestors from a distant mythical land. The annual festivals are well-known, but many ceremonies and observances are performed only by initiates.

Candomblé is based on belief in a supreme deity, Olorum, creator of Obatala (Sky) and Oduluá (Earth), joined in order to give light by Iemanjá (Water) and Aganju (Land). Iemanjá and Aganju have a dishonorable son Orunga (Air). The principal Orixás (gods) connected with Catholic saints are Ogun, god of iron (St. Anthony); Omolu, god of disease (St. Lazarus); Oxumara, a snake, servant of Xangó (St. Bartholomew); Oxóssi, god of the hunt (St. George); Logun Edê, half the year a man and half the year a woman (St. Expeditus); Xangó, god of thunder (St. Jerome); Jansã, goddess of the winds and storms (St. Barbara); Oxum, goddess of the springs and beauty (Our Lady of the Candles); Obá, goddess of the rivers (the last three are wives of the god Xangó). There is also Exu, who is not in the true sense an Orixá, but bears messages between the gods and men.

The *candomblé* ritual begins in the morning with the sacrifice of an animal to the Orixás, in the presence only of initiates, and continues in the afternoon at a public ceremony with songs to the gods accompanied by a group of drummers. Visitors may ask for consultations and advice; Thursday is believed to be the most propitious day.

The *umbanda* cult does not accept original sin but believes that man suffers punishment for an earlier life, so one must struggle for spiritual improvement, adhering to the principles of goodness and charity. In Rio de Janeiro alone 32,000 *umbanda* centers were registered in 1980. It is estimated that Brazil has 30 million followers of *umbanda*, who gather at over 100,000 centers.

Japanese Religions

In June 1908 after sixty days on the sea the ship *Kasato Maru* sailed into the port of Santos with 791 Japanese immigrants. Thus begins the saga of Japanese immigration in Brazil. The group came on the basis of a contract to work on the coffee plantations, hoping to earn enough money and then return to Japan. Instead, they settled permanently in Brazil. Eighty years after the arrival of the first immigrants, the Japanese numbered 1,168,000. The largest concentration is in southeast Brazil — 915,000 (78.3 percent), of which 828,000 are in the state of São Paulo, and about 250,000 in the city of São Paulo.

The Japanese do not have a single religion. Beside regular visits to Shintoist or Buddhist temples, they are interested in numerous sects, for example, Seicho-No-lê (Perfect Liberty), which promises a speedy solution to all problems.

Shintoism, a collection of undefined beliefs, is closely connected with important occasions in life — birth, marriage, the New Year and various others, celebrated in Shintoist shrines. It incorporates worship of various gods and heroes but also deified historical figures — all the emperors who died before 1945, and nature: the sun, moon, water, mountains, etc.

Unlike Shintoism, the religion of the common people, Buddhism was favored by the aristocracy. While for the Japanese Shintoism is a symbol of life, Buddhism symbolizes death and the afterlife. Reverence of ancestors is an important aspect of Buddhism and of numerous other religious movements and sects which developed after the Second World War.

Syncretism accounts for the ability of the Japanese to adapt to dominant religions in the country where they live. It is estimated that 10 percent of Japanese Brazilians attend Catholic and Protestant churches alternately.

The Japanese in Brazil gather for the Flower Festival (*Hana matsuri*) in April, on which occasion Buddhists celebrate the birth of Buddha (April 8); the Star Festival (*Tanabata*) from July 3 to 7, when young Japanese women pray to the stars for success in love; the Festival of the Purification of the Soul (*Oharahi-shiki*) on June 30 and December 31 according to Shintoist tradition; and New Year's Eve (*Motitsuki*) on December 31-January 1. These festivities have helped the Japanese community to preserve the beliefs, cults and philosophy of the Far East in its Brazilian environment.

* * * * *

In this country noted for its religious tolerance and ethnic diversity, many other faiths coexist. Spiritualism has a fairly large following, and there are significant numbers of Eastern Orthodox, Maronites and Muslims.

Di Cavalcanti: cover of the catalogue
of the Modern Art Week Exhibition
held in the Municipal Theater of São
Paulo, February 1922.

Culture

Interwoven Traditions

Many strands have been woven into the colorful tapestry of Brazilian life and culture, but the dominant pattern was set by the Portuguese. It is to Portugal that the great majority of Brazilians owe their language, religion and customs. Though a small country and faced by numerous challenges, it managed to colonize the vast territory of Brazil, to establish an integrated way of life in spite of regional differences, and preserve the unity of its language. But in the shaping of Brazilian culture, as in the formation of a Brazilian identity, a significant role was also played by the native Indians, black Africans and by European and other settlers.

The Portuguese language has been the chief integrating factor since the early years of colonization. As spoken in Brazil, it sounds softer, more melodious than the Portuguese of Europe. Its accent and vocabulary, enriched with words of Indian and African origin, set it off from the language of the mother country, much like the differences between American and British English. Even within Brazil, though, there are differences in the musicality of the spoken language from one part of the country to another. Encouraged by the cordial Brazilians, who will try to understand any level of competence in their language, foreigners do not find Portuguese difficult to learn.

Brazilian culture has been deeply influenced by Roman Catholicism, another basic force of cohesion. In this country with its great variety of faiths, religious tolerance prevails just as the mixture of races resulted in racial tolerance. Though most Brazilians are baptised into the Church of Rome, a large proportion are not practicing Catholics. For many, Catholicism is a kind of social tradition (baptism, marriage, funerals and Sunday Mass).

In time the Amerindians, black Africans and people of mixed ancestry came to accept the Portuguese way of life, adapting it to the environment. Even so, in some parts of the interior the influence of Indian and African culture is still very powerful.

The Indian contribution to the Brazilian cultural heritage is considerable. From the Indians the European settlers learned much about adapting to their new surroundings. Corn, manioc and other crops cultivated by the Indians are still planted. Also in use are ways of fishing and river transportation, cooking utensils and dishes of Indian origin, medicinal herbs and the Indian Tupi language, once widely spoken in the colony. Many Indian names for plants, animals, rivers, places, mountains, have entered into Brazilian Portuguese. Some of these are now used even in English, for example, tapioca and cashew (*acajú*). The Indian contribution is most apparent in the Amazon basin, where rubber-collectors (*seringeiros*) and isolated farmers have preserved many Indian customs and beliefs.

African influence on the Brazilian way of life is strongest in the northeast and along the coast north of Rio de Janeiro. In Salvador, capital of the state of Bahia, a visitor will encounter a series of traditional dishes of African origin, such as *vatapá* (made of manioc flour, coconut oil, fish, shrimps and many spices) and *acarajé* (beancake fried in coconut oil). African rhythms are very much present in Brazilian folk music, especially the samba.

An understanding of these racial, ethnic, religious and regional elements is essential for an appreciation of the spirit of Brazil, its roots, its unity despite diversity. In time, regional differences shaped different types of people. In the north, gathering latex in the Amazon basin, lives the isolated *seringeiro*. The sugar-cane and cacao planters in the northeast also have their specific character, while in the interior lives a type of cowboy, the tough *vaqueiro*, entirely clad in leather as protection from the thorny bushes of the region. Rio de Janeiro is famed for its cosmopolitan charm and its good-looking inhabitants, especially its beautiful women, who open their hearts at carnival time. The energetic people of São Paulo are called the 'Yankees' of Brazil because of their business acumen. The southern state of Rio Grande do Sul is known for its gauchos, the cowboys of the pampas.

Literature

The beginnings of Brazilian literature in the eighteenth century were under the sign of the great Encyclopedists, the French Revolution and the wars for independence in North America. The nineteenth century saw a growing trend toward autonomous literary expression, though the influence of Portugal remained strong. Combining cosmopolitan values and local features, Brazilian literature is a reflection of Brazil's mixed racial and cultural heritage.

Joacquim Maria Machado de Assís (1839-1908), possibly Brazil's greatest novelist, served as the first president of the Brazilian Academy of Letters in 1897. His novel purporting to be the posthumous memoirs of Bras Cubas — *Memórias pósthumas de Bras Cubas* (translated as *The Epitaph of a Small Winner*), published in 1881, provides an unidealized description of the Brazilian scene in the late nineteenth century, given with great depth of psychological observation.

Euclides da Cunha (1866-1909) wrote one of the most influential books in Brazilian literature: *Os sertões* (translated as *Rebellion in the Backlands*), 1902, essential for an understanding of life in northeastern Brazil. For some of the impoverished inhabitants of the Northeast, owing to their miserable living conditions, Catholicism assumed a bizarre form of Messianism. The chief of a poor village in Bahia, Antônio Conselheiro, regarded as a prophet, managed to repulse several police expeditions until finally the entire community was wiped out by the army. Historically true, the episode is brilliantly described in this powerful work.

Jose Pereira de Graça Aranha (1868-1931), a diplomat in Europe for many years, member of the Brazilian Academy of Letters, was preoccupied with the problems of Brazilian civilization, while from Europe he took the latest esthetic and philosophical ideas. In his novel *Canaan*, 1902, he portrays the life of German Pomeranian colonists in the state of Espirito Santo and the conflicts within the Brazilian melting pot.

The works of these authors laid the foundations of a literary movement concerned about the future of Brazil.

Gilberto Freyre (1900-1988) made significant contributions to the study of Brazilian history and to literature. His novel *Casa grande e senzala* (translated as *The Masters and the Slaves*), 1933, is an historical and literary masterpiece about the slave system in the northeast of the country. With this and two other books dealing with the rich and the poor (*Sobrados e mocambos*), 1936, and with order and progress (*Ordem e progresso*), 1959 — Brazil's motto, he completed his analysis of the formation of Brazilian society.

Jorge Amado, born in 1912, is certainly the best known, most popular and most translated Brazilian novelist (some 40 foreign editions). His novels: *Terras do sem fim* (translated as *The Violent Land*), *Gabriela, cravo e canela*, in which the main character, the popular cinnamon-skinned Gabriella smells of cloves, a book about shepherds (*Pastores de Noite*), another about men weary of war (*Tereza Batista cansada da guerra*) and finally a novel about a big ambush (*Tocaia grande a face obscura*), are truly poetic accounts with a serious social content depicting northeastern Brazil and particularly the Brazilians of mixed ancestry who live there.

Carlos Drummond de Andrade (1902-1987) was the first Brazilian poet to gain wide recognition in the post-modern period. His approach is based on a critical, realistic attitude toward himself, toward living beings and objects, the world and society. Literary critics acclaim his work as a high point in Portuguese poetry.

Painting

The first painters of the sixteenth-century colonial period were Jesuit and Benedictine missionaries. With the Dutch expeditions in the mid-seventeenth century came Flemish artists, who painted flora and tropical scenes. Eighteenth-century Brazilian Baroque art reached its zenith during the 'gold cycle' in the cities of Ouro Prêto, Salvador, Recife and Olinda. In the following century artists in Brazil were influenced by successive European trends — late Neo-classicism, Romanticism, Impressionism, and in the early twentieth-century, Academicism and Modernism.

Brazil's best known modern painter and, indeed, the most outstanding Brazilian artist of this century is Cândido Portinari (1903-1962), the son of Italian immigrants. Of special significance was Portinari's decision, before leaving for art school in Paris, to paint only Brazil and its people, a promise he kept until the end of his life. After his return from Paris he developed into a painter of social themes, producing work so outstanding that some critics divide the history of Brazilian painting into two periods: before and after Portinari.

Just as Michelangelo in *The Last Judgement* in the Sistine Chapel included a disagreeable priest he knew among the figures in Hell, Portinari in one of his best known paintings, *Tiradentes* (tempera on canvas, 3.15 × 18.00 m., Bandeirante Palace, São Paulo, 1949), gave this immortal hero of Brazilian independence the likeness of Brazilian communist leader Luis Carlos Prestes, a friend of his.

His large murals were influenced by Italian painters of the fourteenth and fifteenth centuries, especially Giotto and Piero della Francesca, and by the Mexican muralist, Diego de Rivera. At the U.N. headquarters in

New York the two front walls (280 sq.m.) of the delegates' entrance were reserved for a Brazilian contribution. Their decoration was assigned to Portinari, who selected the theme and from 1952 until 1956 worked on two murals, *War* and *Peace* (oils on wood, 14.00 × 10.00 m.).

In his later work this highly prolific artist abandoned dramatic social themes for important historical subjects, beginning with the discovery of Brazil.

Sculpture

The finest sculptor and one of the best architects of the colonial period in Brazil was Antônio Francisco Lisboa, generally known as Aleijadinho, son of a Portuguese architect and an African slave. His numerous works, essentially Baroque with elements of Rococo and other expressionist features, represent the peak of Brazilian colonial art. Many of his carvings were in soft soapstone. His last works, judged master-pieces, were the statues of twelve prophets, carved between 1800 and 1805, which stand in front of the church of Bom Jesus de Matosinho in Congonhas do Campo (Minas Gerais). The church with its six chapels was modeled after the church of Bom Jesus de Braga in Portugal. The name of Aleijadinho ('the little cripple') remains inseparably linked with the Brazilian Baroque and its famous churches.

Modern Architecture

The Brazilian school of modern architecture, skillfully adapted to the country's climate, is world-renowned. Modern architecture in Brazil traces its beginnings to the middle of the first half of this century in São Paulo. The Modern Art Week celebrated in this city in February 1922 is seen as a turning-point in Brazilian literature, painting, sculpture, architecture and music. As an original movement, a tropical version of the so-called International Style, modern architecture actually stemmed from Rio de Janeiro, which regrettably has few examples designed by Brazil's greatest names in this field.

The beginnings of modern Brazilian architecture are also associated with the visit of Le Corbusier, whose principles of town-planning were based on the well-being of man, on social and economic reality and modern technology. His ideas and work greatly influenced younger Brazilian architects, among them Oscar Niemeyer, who became a friend of Le Corbusier and his most faithful disciple. Born in Rio de Janeiro in 1909, Niemeyer is recognized as one of the most outstanding figures of world twentieth-century architecture.

150.
Harvesting sugar cane in São Paulo state, which provides nearly half the country's sugar output.

151.
A coffee plantation in São Paulo state. After the abolition of slavery and the arrival of more European immigrants, the center of the coffee industry moved to this region. ▸

152.
A soybean field in the state of Mato Grosso, where cultivation of this crop began in the mid-nineteenth century.▸ ▸

153.
Vast tracts in Mato Grosso have been converted into grazing land. Ranches raising thousands of head of cattle have made this region the country's major meat producer. ▸ ▸ ▸

154.
A fazenda at Itamaratí (Mato Grosso do Sul), one of many such large estates engaged in mixed crop production.

155

155.
Rice-growing in the valley of the Rio São Francisco in northeastern Brazil. Introduced in the early eighteenth century, rice has become a staple of the diet, and is now raised on nearly five million hectares.

156

156, 157, 158.
Sugar-cane harvesters in São Paulo
state take a rest from their
backbreaking work. First grown in
Brazil in the mid-sixteenth century,
sugar cane was the mainstay of the
colony's prosperity for some 200
years. At that time the northeast was
the center of sugar production,
concentrated in the hands of a
relatively few wealthy families, the
great plantation owners.

157

159

159.
A cotton field in São Paulo state.
This crop, now covering over 3.5
million hectares, was first raised on
small farms in the eighteenth century,
later becoming also a large plantation
crop, as in North America.

160, 161.
Cutting sugar cane is thirsty work. In
the past it was done mainly by
African slaves, first brought over
primarily to supply labor for the
sugar-cane plantations of the
northeast, since the native Indians
were too few and often unamenable.

162-165.
Amazonia has a bewildering variety and abundance of fruits and nuts, among them the Brazil nut (naturally enough), the large Brazilian avocado, the jaca and the coconut.

167.
Harvesting latex from a rubber tree. The great boom in this commodity in the nineteenth century brought immense wealth to plantation owners, who spent it lavishly in and on such cities as Manaus and Belém. The Portuguese learned about rubber-tapping from the Indians.

166.
A coconut vendor with his donkey.

168.
A Belém beauty cools off with a refreshing drink of coconut milk. ▶

The construction of the new capital, Brasília, was begun in 1957. Innovatively planned by Lúcio Costa, it is the only modern city included in UNESCO's world heritage list. Costa's *plano piloto* was suggestive of an airplane, a symbol of progress and national integration. The most important buildings in Brasília were designed by Niemeyer: the president's palace — Palácio do Planalto, the presidential residence — Palácio Alvorada, the Palace of the National Congress, the Supreme Court building, the Ministry of Foreign Affairs — Palácio dos Arcos (Itamaratí), the central piazza — Praça dos Três Poderes, the Tancredo Neves Pantheon dedicated to all who fought for freedom and democracy in Brazil, and the cathedral of Brasília, one of the most remarkable examples of modern religious architecture in the world.

The Latin American Memorial raised in São Paulo in 1989 as, in the architect's words, "an act of continental faith and solidarity", was also designed by Oscar Niemeyer.

Burle Marx, Brazil's best known landscaper, has played an important role in modern Brazilian architecture, harmonizing horizontal settings of greenery with vertical buildings of cement, steel and glass.

The famous church of São Francisco de Assis at Pampulha, Belo Horizonte, in the state of Minas Gerais was designed by Oscar Niemeyer and Burle Marx and decorated with paintings, frescoes and wall tiles by Cândido Portinari. Bearing in mind Le Corbusier's tenets, Niemeyer designed a section of Pampulha (the casino, yachting club, dance hall and church) with such freedom of form that it is considered a landmark in the development of modern architecture.

Music

Among the highlights of Modern Art Week in February 1922 in São Paulo were performances of the works of composer Heitor Villa-Lobos (1887-1959), later to achieve international renown. His work, traditional in form, includes seven operas, twelve symphonies, five ballets, thirteen symphonic poems, five concertos for piano and orchestra, seventeen string quartets and numerous other pieces. He mainly owes his fame, however, to his most original works, his nine *Bachianas Brásileiras* and fourteen *Chôros*, in which he incorporated black African and Amerindian folk music. He elevated Brazilian national awareness to a high level of artistic expression by mingling a vigorous cultural heritage with elements still surviving in remote parts of Brazil.

* * * * *

There can be few countries in the world where folk music plays a more pervasive role in national life and culture. Its exciting rhythms and haunting melodies echo the diversity of the Brazilian cultural heritage — Portuguese, Indian and a strong African note. In a country with a large number of illiterates it was also the best means of mass communication.

From the 1930s onward the carnival gave a strong impetus to the creation of popular music and performers alike, participating year after year in this popular festival. The generation of the 1960s, which produced the best-known Brazilian performers of popular-folk music, formed part of an international movement that used music to express political consciousness and self-awareness.

At the Rio carnival of 1917 a new rhythm was launched with the performance of the first Brazilian samba: *Pelo telefone* (Telephone). The 1930s came to be called the Golden Age of Brazilian popular music, particularly the samba, which conquered Europe and North America.

The best-known Brazilian singer of all time, Carmen Miranda (her real name Maria do Carmo Miranda da Cunha), shot to fame with her interpretation of the song *Tai* (a nickname) at the 1929 carnival. The vivacious star of many Hollywood musicals in the Forties, she was famous for her fiery temperament and the stylized version of the Bahia costume she made her 'trademark'.

Following the samba, Brazilian composers of popular music produced the bossa nova, combining traditional Brazilian folk music and the harmonies of American jazz. Antonio Carlos Jobim, composer of the popular *Garota da Ipanema* (Girl from Ipanema) and also Miles Davis and Gil Evans were all influenced to some extent by Debussy, Stravinsky and Bartok. For a time, in the late Fifties and early Sixties, this new dance eclipsed the samba in popularity in Brazil and abroad. But the traditional samba, with innovations, soon regained its place as Brazil's favorite, and has retained it ever since.

Heritage of Mankind

Brazilian cities with outstanding monuments of Baroque art and architecture have been proclaimed by UNESCO as part of the cultural heritage of mankind: 1. the historic center of Olinda in the state of Pernambuco; 2. the historic center of Salvador (Bahia); 3. the historic center of Ouro Prêto (Minais Gerais); 4. the church of Bom Jesus de Matozinho in Congonhas do Campo (Minas Gerais) with its statues of twelve prophets — a masterpiece of colonial art by sculptor Aleijadinho.

The list continues: 5. the Jesuit missions for the Guarani Indians — remains of churches and villages built by the Jesuits in the second half of the seventeenth century in Rio Grande do Sul, on the border between Brazil and Argentina; 6. the National Park of Iguaçu with its scenic wonder, the Iguaçu Falls, in the state of Paraná on the border between Brazil, Argentina and Paraguay.

And finally: 7. the capital city of Brasília, actually its central urban plan (*Plano piloto*).

Georg Marcgraf: 'Sugar Mill', engraving in the book 'Historia Naturalis Braziliae', National Library, Rio de Janeiro.

Life and Leisure

National Characteristics

Love of life, a passion for speed, rhythm and color, a deep appreciation of beauty — these are all part of the Brazilian make-up. Spontaneous, cordial people, Brazilians are noted for their sense of humor and delight in telling jokes about the Portuguese or hearing Portuguese jokes about themselves, neither sparing the other.

Naturally they have a more serious side. Brazilians love their country, though ever ready to criticize the nation's politics. A certain sense of inferiority that the average Brazilian used to feel with respect to industrially advanced states has now given way to a feeling of belonging to a big, richly-endowed, developing country which believes in its future. This is the natural consequence of the country's rapid growth and the increasingly important role that Brazil plays in Latin America and the world.

Brazil boasts first-rate specialists, trained at Brazilian and the leading universities of the U.S.A. and Western Europe. This intellectual élite, which can hold its own with experts in developed countries, includes researchers in scientific institutes, university professors, diplomats, businessmen, engineers, architects, physicians, civil servants and, of course, artists of international fame. The Brazilians' spontaneity springs from their pragmatism, from a practical spirit without religious, political, or ideological prejudices. They realized early that a developing country could progress more rapidly through economic, scientific, cultural and technological cooperation with the advanced states. They have studied and taken advantage of the experience of others in all domains, from the raising of corn and soybeans to communications, the parliamentary system and other institutions.

Brazil participated in the First and Second World Wars on the side of the Allies, the soldiers and officers of the Brazilian Expeditionary Corps fighting bravely on the Allied front in Italy, 1944-1945. Officers have traditionally enjoyed considerable social status, and military service is obligatory. Brazilians, however, are not militarists by temperament, despite (or because of) lengthy periods under military regimes. They are peace-loving, tolerant people, not disposed to aggression.

One of the essential characteristics of the Brazilians is their great affection for the family. Young people treat their parents with great tenderness and respect, and all Brazilians love children. Families tend to be closely knit and patriarchal. The average Brazilian woman cares for her husband very diligently, discreetly remaining in the background, satisfied that she is thus contributing to her husband's success. This does not mean that Brazilian women feel inferior or have few interests outside the family. Many of them are very active, particularly in humanitarian and other organizations. There are distinguished women scientists, artists, university professors, doctors, journalists, and even members of Congress and the government.

The beauty of the country, the amiability and friendliness of its people, seem destined to live in harmony.

Food and Drink

Brazilians have a hearty appreciation of the good things of life, among which they count food and drink. Thanks to its climate and geographical features, the country has a great variety and abundance of farm produce, as well as sea and river fish.

The staple foods in the Brazilian diet are beans and rice. Though each region has its specialities, the *feijoada completa* is regarded as the national dish. It can be prepared in several ways, but the chief ingredients are always beans and rice, combined with pork, pig's ears, sun-dried meat (*carne de sol*) or sausages, and plenty of pepper. It is served with slices of orange, fried manioc flour, a spicy pimento sauce called *malagueta* and a mixture of boiled vegetables.

The most popular regional dishes are: turtle soup, duck prepared in the Indian manner in a special manioc sauce (*pato na tucupi*); lobster or shrimps in coconut sauce; sea crab baked in its shell (*casquinha de siri*); *carne de sol*, and grilled meat (*churrasco*). Salvador (Bahia) is noted for its dishes of African origin: *moqueca de peixe* (fish or mussels simmered in oil and pepper); *xinxim de galinha* (ragout of chicken with onion, garlic, palm oil, shrimps and pumpkin pips); *vatapá* made of fish, shrimps, meat, palm oil, peppers and manioc flour. As an aperitif one takes a glass of *caipirinha*, a cocktail made of sugar-cane brandy (*cachaca*), lemon juice, sugar and ice, which is one of the most popular alcoholic drinks. For dessert there are oranges or a Brazilian favorite, white cheese (*gueijo de Minas*) served with guava jelly, popularly called Romeo and Juliet.

The national drink, needless to say, is coffee, consumed in quantities appropriate to the country which is the world's largest producer.

Soccer

Soccer was introduced by the British, who could never have guessed that the Brazilians would one day surpass them at their national sport. The victory of the Brazilian soccer team in four World Cups — Sweden in 1958, Chile in 1962, Mexico in 1970 and U.S.A. in 1994 — has confirmed the superiority of the attractive, imaginative Brazilian game. The World Cup in Sweden featured a remarkably talented eighteen-year-old player, Edson Arantes do Nascimiento, better known as Pelé, one of the greatest soccer players of all time. When Pelé scored his one thousandth goal, he retired with full honors at Rio's Maracanã stadium.

Brazilians are passionate fans, encouraging their favorites with songs, musical instruments, flag-waving and, outside the stadium, by setting off fireworks. Despite all this frenetic excitemet, on the field Brazilian players are gentlemen. While they try to impress their fans with brilliant ball-control and beautifully-scored goals, the spectators, as if led by a conductor, cheer and urge on their team to greater heights. The whole stadium appears to pulsate for all ninety minutes of play. But when the game is over, the crowd files out in an orderly fashion, without shoving or pushing, regardless of the outcome of the game.

In 1950, when Brazil lost the World Cup final to Uruguay at the newly opened Maracanã stadium, the whole country was in mourning. Some of the more excitable fans even suffered heart attacks. The Maracanã, built in record time for this event, has a crowd capacity of 200,000. Every city in Brazil has its own large stadium seating thousands of spectators.

The celebrity, even adulation, and financial rewards of soccer stardom make it the dream of Brazilian boys from the poorer classes. They can be seen honing their skills in improvised games on the beaches, empty lots and streets of the big cities, in the hope of becoming another Garrincha or Pelé, but also from pure love of the sport.

Carnival

African music and dance have been present in Brazil ever since the coming of the first African slaves in the early days of colonization. Still, it was three centuries before African music was widely accepted and gained entrance to the salons of Rio de Janeiro and other big cities.

The Angolan tam-tam provided the basis for the choreography and music of the samba, the most popular Brazilian rhythm, famous largely because of Brazil's biggest and most spectacular folk festival — the Rio carnival.

The origins of the carnival go back to festivals held in the Azores in the fifteenth and sixteenth centuries, and brought to Rio at the beginning of the colonial period.

The poor, for a long time excluded from clubs, organized their own carnival societies. Some of them became well-known, for example, the *Cordão da Bola Preta*, which to this day traditionally opens the carnival in Rio. The group bears a standard with a white background and a black ball in the middle.

The first large-scale carnival was held in Rio in 1854. Advertisements invited everyone, both rich and poor, to take part. The committee entrusted with its organization included lawyers, doctors, journalists, civil servants, businessmen and officers. In 1870 'big societies' were formed for participating in the program, and remained active until the appearance of the 'samba schools' (*escolas de samba*), now the greatest attraction at the Rio carnival. The first of these (*Deixa falar*) was founded in 1928. In the early years they performed without official status; in 1932, the first year they took part in the competition, the winner was the *Estação Primeira de Mangueira* samba school. By the Fifties the samba schools were well organized, and the institution has survived, with certain modifications, until the present day.

The star of the carnival is the poor mulatto girl of the *favelas* of Rio. For 364 days people practice in the samba schools, dreaming of the one night in the year when they become queens and kings, princesses and princes in glittering costumes. Then thousands leave their hovels in the *favelas* and commit themselves body and soul to the carnival spirit. Briefly, the hardships of their daily lives are forgotten as they enter into the roles assigned to them in the samba schools and the carnival program.

During the carnival the beautiful mulatto celebrated by famous Brazilian poets, composers and painters — seems to be a symbol of beauty and racial democracy. For the three days of the celebration Rio de Janeiro and all of Brazil, particularly the Northeast, sing and dance; everyone is a friend in a kind of imaginary human fraternity. Some spend an entire year's savings.

The carnival mood is perhaps best expressed by the words of the samba *Felicidade* from the film *Black Orpheus*:

> "Sorrow knows no end...
> Happiness, yes!
> The happiness of a poor man is
> The great illusion of the carnival.
> People work all year long
> For a moment of fancy,
> To become in their fantasies
> King, corsair or gardener,
> And it all ends on Wednesday..."

The melody and lyrics of each new samba are important topics of conversation. Composers of popular music in Rio and Brazil are idols, and not only among the young. Everybody recognizes them on the streets of Rio and shows their respect.

The carnival program begins on Sunday evening and ends on Shrove Tuesday. Filing through the center of Rio, the samba schools are judged on the *Passarela do Samba*, i.e. the *Sambódromo*, 650 yards long with 60,000 seats, arranged on both sides of the street. The competition between the samba schools is fierce, and the jury's marks final. Each samba school representing a part of the city selects its melody and program — the color scheme, costumes and artistic interpretation of the theme. All this is a jealously guarded secret at the samba school as it prepares all year long for the great event. Some of the schools send 3000 or 4000 participants to the festival.

The *Passarela do Samba* (*Sambódromo*), inaugurated at the carnival of 1984, was designed by Brazil's most distinguished architect, Oscar Niemeyer.

Unlike other big cities, where folk festivals are gradually dying out, Rio vigorously promotes its carnival, which has become almost synonymous with the city, and attracts tourists from all over the world.

Festival of the Water Goddess

As one year passes into another, Rio de Janeiro and the whole Northeast do honor to the African goddess of water, Iemanjá. On the evening between December 31 and January 1 the beaches of Rio — Copacabana, Ipanema, Leblon — are filled with hundreds of thousands of people of every social class, come out of curiosity or to take part in festivities consisting of prayer, song, dance and rituals.

The crowds on the beaches of Rio de Janeiro, Salvador and other cities sing and dance around blazing bonfires, and at midnight small boats laden with gifts head out to sea to appease the water goddess. Brazilians well know that, even in the computer age, man is no match for the elemental forces of nature, which still reign supreme over much of their great land.

Distinguished Brazilians

Antônio Francisco Lisboa - Aleijadinho (1730-1814)

The son a Portuguese architect, Manuel Francisco Lisboa, and a black slave named Isabel, Aleijadinho ('the little cripple') inherited from his father his feeling for art, especially the Baroque, and from his mother, perhaps, an African affinity for expressionist sculpture. Growing up during the gold-rush era in Minas Gerais, he acquired his knowledge of art and architecture from his father and uncle, Antônio Francisco Pombal, and his training in sculpture and carving from the artists Francisco Xavier de Brito and José Coelho de Naronha.

The greatest artist of Brazil's colonial period, he gained his knowledge of world art through books and illustrations, for he never traveled outside Minas Gerais, apart from one trip to Rio de Janeiro.

Though also a gifted architect, he is better known for his sculpture, particularly his inspired figures of twelve Old Testament prophets before the church of Bom Jesus de Matozinho in Congonhas do Campo (Minas Gerais). Carved in soapstone between 1800 and 1805, they form an entity of great beauty and dramatic expressiveness.

José Bonafacío de Adrada e Silva (1763-1838)

Born into a prominent colonial family in Santos, he went to study at the University of Coimbra in Portugal and remained there as a professor. One of the most outstanding scientists of his age, with an international reputation as a naturalist and geologist, he returned to Brazil at the age of fifty-eight and entered political life, becoming one of its most powerful figures.

Before the proclamation of independence, on September 7, 1822, the Prince Regent named him Minister of Foreign Affairs. In this position he exerted a strong influence, persuading Don Pedro to remain in Brazil and declare it independent of Portugal. For this reason he became known as the 'Patriarch of Independence'.

Andrada e Silva made a decisive contribution toward the consolidation of the new state in a very short time. He was instrumental in organizing the army and navy, adapting the administration to the new system, compelling the Portuguese garrisons to leave Brazil, and ensuring diplomatic recognition of the state. The U.S.A. officially recognized Brazil in 1824, and Portugal and Great Britain followed in 1825.

However, Andrada e Silva soon came into conflict with the absolutist conceptions of Emperor Pedro I when it came to drawing up the Constitution, and joined the opposition in Parliament. After the emperor's abdication, he was tutor to the young Pedro II.

Joaquim Maria Machado de Assís (1839-1908)

Born as a mestizo into a poor family, orphaned early and suffering from epilepsy from childhood, it is astonishing that Machado de Assís should have attained such eminence in life. While learning four or five languages, he earned his living by publishing articles, stories, poems and serialized novels in the daily press and magazines.

Machado de Assís was most responsible for the foundation of the Brazilian Academy of Letters, of which he became the first president in 1897. Many critics consider him Brazil's greatest novelist. His first literary efforts were romantic poems, and his early novels were tinged with romanticism. But the publication in 1881 of the novel *Memórias Póstumas de Brás Cubas* (*The Epitaph of a Small Winner*) saw his emergence as a mature writer and the coming-of-age of the Brazilian novel in general. It marks a break with the earlier idealized description of urban life. Machado de Assís also wrote noted works on the theater and literary criticism. The influence of English (Sterne, Swift), French and German writers can be detected in his work.

José Maria de Silva Paronhas Júnior, Baron of Rio Branco (1845-1912)

The Baron of Rio Branco, statesman and historian, came from one of the most prominent Brazilian families which produced a number of leading politicians and statesmen in the nineteenth and twentieth centuries. He early on showed a talent for historical and geographical studies, particularly military history. Journalist, parliamentary deputy and diplomat, he was appointed Foreign Minister in 1902 and held the post until his death in 1912.

Thanks to his erudition and diplomatic skill, he succeeded in resolving by treaty all border questions with Brazil's neighbors (Bolivia, Peru, etc.). To commemorate his services in the acquisition of the territory of the present federal state of Acre in Amazonia, when the frontier with Bolivia was demarcated, the state capital was named Rio Branco.

The academy attached to the Brazilian Ministry of Foreign Affairs, which prepares future diplomats is called the Rio Branco Institute.

169.
Prospectors like these in Cotia (Pará state) are now seeking gold in the Amazon. Some old fields in Minas Gerais, first exploited in the eighteenth century, are still being worked, though many are exhausted.

170.
Miners in Serra Pelada (Pará). Gold was discovered in the Amazon basin in the 70s. By 1985 the region had yielded 35.3 tons. Exploitation of the gold-bearing areas has had disastrous consequences for the Indians whose territory has been invaded by prospectors. ▶

171.
Miners in Serra Pelada (Pará). The output of this field declined from 6.6 tons of gold in 1980 to under one ton in 1989. About 25,000 prospectors are at work here. ▶ ▶

172.
A prospector in Cotia (Pará) lugging·
ore. Whatever gold he finds must be
sold to a government-controled
agency. It is estimated that in earlier
years at least half the gold found was
smuggled out of the fields. Stricter
vigilance and checks have cut down
on this.

173.
Gold prospecting in Cotia (Pará).
Only a few have grown rich by
turning up a large nugget. If a man
finds one, it is wiser to conceal it
from other miners.

174.
Most of the Amazonian gold-seekers
are impoverished peasants from the
northeast trying to make a living.

175.
Gold miners in Cotia (Pará). When a
rich vein is struck, poor miners are
soon joined by others, even college
graduates, hoping to get rich quick.

176.
The prospectors are mostly
Brazilians, but a few slip across the
border from Bolivia or Columbia.
Their total number in Amazonia has
been estimated at half a million.

177.
A gold miner or garimpeiro in Serra
Pelada (Pará). The death rate is high
as a result of accidents, especially
landslides, and the 'law of the jungle'
which prevails among the
prospectors.

178.
A mining camp (Cotia, Pará).
Because of the deplorable living
conditions, disease, especially
malaria, is rife. The turnover of the
labor force is understandably high.

179.
Prospectors (Cotia, Pará) stubbornly
resist the use of machinery in the gold
fields, preferring to trust to their own
luck.

180.
Panning for gold in Cotia (Pará).
Beside digging, Amazonian gold-
seekers also use the old method of
sifting the precious metal from river
mud. Gold was panned in the
colonial period, but digging produces
higher yields.

181, 182.
Since panning is less physically
demanding than digging, it is often
done by boys. In the first few years,
the yield from the Pará gold fields
was equal to that during the
eighteenth-century gold rush.

181

182

247

183-186.
Prospectors in the Amazon are mainly mestizos, with a sprinkling of hardy whites. Living and working under appalling conditions, they stretch themselves to the limits of human endurance to provide for their families or in hope of a future life of luxury.

187-190.
The garimpeiros are a tough breed
prepared to risk their lives daily,
though the chance of making a
fortune is slim. Some are reckless
adventurers, others just desperately
needy.

191

191, 192.
Few bring their families to the gold fields. Wives and children come for only brief visits since there are no facilities for a longer stay. In some areas visitors are not permitted, and in any case access is extremely difficult.

192

196, 197.
No one can be trusted. Prospectors keep a close eye on the agent weighing the gold. From their earnings they must pay high prices for groceries and other necessities flown in by bush pilots, and sold at makeshift 'supermercados'. Local peasants also profit by their needs. ▶ ▶

198, 199.
Entertainment in the jungle — playing pool or watching a mud-wrestling match between camp followers. The barman, too, will take his cut of the prospectors' earnings. ▶ ▶ ▶

193, 194.
The garimpeiro must be something of a gambler by nature, and gambling is one of his few forms of relaxation in the Amazon wilds. The money he gets from his hard-earned gold dust, weighed out by the gram, is often lost the same night.

195.
Mining camps shelter poverty-stricken peasants simply trying to support a family, but also trigger-happy speculators. Fights and theft are commonplace, violent death not rare. ▶

193

200.
A prospector dozing in his hammock, dreaming perhaps of a comfortable bed in Rio or São Paulo.

201.
The Amazon jungle, home to a million species of animal and plant life, is in jeopardy through the activities of just one — Homo sapiens. An estimated 12,350 square miles of Brazilian rain forest — an area larger than Belgium — was consumed by fire in 1988 alone, while dam and road construction and other projects threaten the jungle's ecosystem.

202.
Aerial view of Amazonia. The Amazon rain forest (selvas) is the most extensive in the world. Its further destruction by burning and felling could have disastrous consequences for global weather. ▶

203.
The Rio Tiquie meandering through the Amazon jungle. The Amazon basin drains the largest volume of water in the world, a fifth of the earth's fresh water resources. ▶▶

204.
The Rio Tiquie, one of the Amazon's one thousand tributaries. Heavy rains, high humidity, and, as in all jungles, a poor soil make farming here unhealthy and unprofitable. When stripped of its trees, the land proves ill-suited to agriculture. ▶▶▶

205.
The confluence of the Solimões and
Negro rivers near Manaus, five miles
wide. At this point the bluish-black
waters of the Rio Negro mix with the
brownish-yellow Rio Solimões.

206.
An Indian family paddling down the
Solimões. As most travel is by water,
the people of the Amazon usually
build their homes on river banks.

207.
A tiny boat on a wide expanse of
water near Belém (Pará). The main
port for Amazon craft, Belém lies
some 80 miles up the Pará River from
the Atlantic.

208, 209, 210.
'Amazonian' is the very word to
describe much of the plant life of this
region, with its gigantic trees soaring
to 200 feet, and the Victoria regia lily,
its pads reaching up to six feet in
diameter and capable of supporting a
weight of 154 pounds. Botanists have
still to classify much of the Amazon's
unique flora. The chance may be lost
forever if the destruction of the selvas
continues unchecked.

211.
The canoe is the only possible means
of transport through the intricate
maze of channels branching off the
rivers of Amazonia.

212.
Indians of the Yanomami tribe
skinning alligators at Missao de
Maturaća (Amazonia).

213

The Indian village known as Missao de Maturaća in northern Amazonia is inhabited by members of the Yanomami tribe, whose traditional land is intersected by the Brazil-Venezuela border.

213

214.
A man holding a water snake near Manaus (Amazonia). The jungle is full of different kinds of snakes, among them some of the world's biggest — the Amazonian anaconda — and most venomous — the coral and urutu.

214

215.
A family in the Yanomami village of
Missao de Maturaća. In the last few
years, since the arrival of gold
prospectors in the area, this tribe,
once numbering some 9000, has been
decimated by malaria.

215

216.
A Yanomami hunter testing his
blowpipe, Missao de Maturaća
(Amazonia).

217.
Yanomami children are just as much at home on water as on land. From a tender age they are taught the traditional skills of their tribe.

218.
A Yanomami woman and child at Missao de Maturaća. In Mato Grosso and Amazonia many missions, both Catholic and Protestant, bring education and medical care to the Indians. The Church is often in the forefront of the struggle to protect the natives from exploitation and displacement from their territory.

219.
The Indian of the Amazon is unmatched in skill as a hunter with arrow, spear and blowpipe. The tribes of hunter-gatherers are rapidly shrinking as 'civilized' man encroaches on their homelands.

220, 222.
The survival of the remaining Amazonian Indians is threatened by diseases such as measles and malaria brought by developers, settlers and prospectors.

221.
Luscious fruits of the Amazon.

223.
Clearing the forest, whether for farming or ranching, has produced less prosperity than expected. The nutrient-poor soil is soon exhausted, and many pioneer settler families give up or have to move on to clear new land.

223

224, 225.
Since 1973 the Trans-Amazon Highway, 3100 miles in length, has linked up the eastern and westernmost points of Amazonia. It intersects the main north-south road connecting Belém with Brasília, opening up the interior for settlement and economic development.

224

226.
Helicopters are essential for flying
supplies into the Amazonian
wilderness, needing less landing space
than winged craft. In some areas they
are the main means of
communication with the outside
world.

226

227.
Drilling for oil in the Amazon has yielded encouraging results, supporting forecasts that by the mid-90s the country will be self-sufficient in oil.

228.
The construction of landing strips in the jungle is part of the program of establishing communications in an extremely inaccessible region.

229.
Children in the devastated jungle of the Amazon. Uncontroled cutting and burning of the rain forest and other activities pursued by multinational companies have seriously disturbed the ecological balance in some areas.

229

Gentúlio Dornellas Vargas (1883-1954)

Vargas, considered the most important president in Brazilian history, was born at São Borja (Rio Grande do Sul) into a politically influential family, and practiced law before entering politics. He was elected state governor in 1928 and after an unsuccessful bid to be elected president, in 1930 assumed power after a coup. This marked the beginning of the Second Republic.

Unlike previous presidents he sought working-class support, initiating populist policies. He recognized the labor unions and placed them under state control, stabilized conditions of employment, introduced pensions and annual holidays with pay, but did not permit strikes.

In his first fifteen years of authoritarian rule (1930-1945) Vargas cleaned up the corrupt administration, replaced all the state governors, abolished the right of the federal states to levy taxes, and restricted some of the privileges of the two economically most important states, São Paulo and Minas Gerais, all aimed at creating a uniform Brazilian policy.

The 1937 Constitution violated the principle of harmony and independence of the 'three powers', for President Vargas controled the legislative and judicial branches. He was driven out of office in 1945 but, enjoying wide support among the working people, he was elected president in regular fashion in 1950. In his second term he respected civil rights, aided the unions, and strengthened the state's role in the economy. But inflation and other problems led to a fresh crisis and President Vargas, pressed to resign, committed suicide.

Heitor Villa-Lobos (1887-1959)

The best-known and most prolific of Brazilian composers, Villa-Lobos wrote in many different musical forms. From the age of eighteen he traveled around Brazil collecting several thousand folk melodies, some of which he incorporated in his own compositions.

From 1923 to 1930 he lived in Paris, where he associated with the greatest composers and artists of the time (Milhaud, Varèse, Picasso, Stravinsky, Prokofiev). His works were performed by the celebrated pianist Arthur Rubenstein. From Paris he traveled around Europe and Latin America, establishing himself as one of the leading composers of the American continent.

On his return to Brazil he devoted himself to promoting musical education and activity, especially among the young, founding the Brazilian Academy of Music in 1945. Villa-Lobos spent the last years of his life in the U.S.A., mostly New York, where he continued to compose tirelessly. He was awarded an honorary doctorate by New York University. Even in the very last year of his life he still served as member of the jury of the Pablo Casals International Competition in Mexico.

230.
Burnt forest, a posthumous memorial
to the agony of nature and a warning
for the future.

Emiliano Augusto Cavalcanti de Albuquerque Melo - Di Cavalcanti (1897-1976)

Known as an artist by the name Di Cavalcanti, he first published his sketches in the press as early as 1914, and in 1917 had a one-man exhibition of his caricatures. He played a prominent part in the Modern Art Week in São Paulo in 1922. Living in Paris for some years, he associated with the poets Jean Cocteau and Blais Cendrars, the writer Miguel de Unamuno, and the painters Picasso, Braque, Léger and Matisse. His work was influenced by Expressionism, Cubism and Surrealism. After traveling in Italy, where he discovered "the colors of Titian and the theatrical power of Michelangelo", he exhibited in Brussels, London, Amsterdam, Berlin, Lisbon and Paris. He went back to Brazil but soon returned to Paris (1935-1940).

The Thirties is the period of Di Cavalcanti's full artistic maturity. His works are mostly Brazilian in theme, with large, sensual figures of mulatto women. One of his best known is *Five Girls from Guaratingueta* (1930).

Juscelino Kubitschek de Oliveira (1902-1976)

Probably the most popular president of Brazil, Kubitschek was a physician, deputy, mayor of Belo Horizonte and governor of Minas Gerais before his election as president in 1956. As governor he showed himself an able administrator and organizer of dynamic economic growth (building of five hydroelectric power stations, 2000 miles of roads, etc.).

On becoming president he inaugurated a program of rapid development ("Fifty years in five"), especially in the interior. He encouraged the expansion of shipbuilding, the automobile industry, steel and power production. His program for developing the Northeast was accompanied by economic and social welfare measures.

Kubitschek's name is indivisibly linked with that of Brasília, to which he contributed so much. Work on it began in earnest in 1957 and the new capital was inaugurated on April 20, 1960, on the anniversary of the execution of Brazil's national hero, Joaquim José da Silva Xavier-Tiradentes in 1792.

Kubitschek's term of office expired in 1960.

Carlos Drummond de Andrade (1902-1987)

After studying pharmacy at his parents' wish, he followed his literary bent, writing for newspapers in Rio de Janeiro, and worked in the Ministry of Education. Drummond de Andrade, considered Brazil's greatest contemporary poet, was the first major postmodernist to gain a reputation. His view of life, himself, and reality expressed in his work is colored by a profound scepticism. He belongs to the 'Generation of 1930', a group of poets whose work is freer in its subjects and permeated with philosophical reflections and anxiety over the economic and political situation. He was already a well-known poet when Karl Jaspers and Jean-Paul Sartre were just starting out to explore Existentialism.

Lúcio Costa (born 1902)

Born in Toulouse, France, he studied architecture at the National School of Fine Arts in Rio de Janeiro and in 1931 became its principal. Costa has made a major contribution to the preservation of Brazil's artistic heritage and to modern architecture. He designed in 1934 the notable building of the Ministry of Education, which after consultation with Le Corbusier he built in 1943. Its design and constructional solutions had a strong impact on the subsequent course of modern Brazilian architecture.

Costa has received an honorary doctorate from Harvard University (1960), the Calouste Gulbenkian Prize, and the medal of the French Legion of Honor. At the invitation of the Italian government, he took part in consultations regarding the future urban planning of Florence after the 1964 flood.

Lúcio Costa is best known, however, as the author of the *Plano piloto* for Brasília, considered the greatest urban planning project of modern times.

Cândido Portinari Torquato (1903-1962)

The son of an Italian immigrant, Portinari showed his talent for painting as a boy, and helped to restore the church decoration in his native place in the state of São Paulo. Having graduated from the National School of Fine Arts in Rio de Janeiro, he left to continue his studies in Paris in 1929, spending his days in museums and galleries and his evenings at the theater. While in London in the latter half of 1930, he was particularly impressed by the huge canvases of Veronese in the National Gallery. After traveling also in Italy, he became home-sick and, as he later said, "discovered Brazil in Paris". He returned in 1931 determined to devote himself exclusively to Brazilian subjects.

Portinari made his mark internationally by winning a prize for his painting *Coffee* at the 1935 Pittsburg International Exhibition sponsored by the Carnegie Institute. Under the influence of the Mexican muralists, he executed large panels for the building of the Ministry of Education in Rio de Janeiro (1937-1945).

In the Forties his work was mostly in the social expressionist vein, but toward the end of the decade and in the Fifties he also painted historical subjects: *The First Mass in Brazil* (1948), *Tiradentes* (1949) and *War and Peace* (1957).

Oscar Niemeyer (born 1907)

After graduating in architecture at the National School of Fine Arts in his native Rio de Janeiro in 1934, he worked for a time in the studio of Lúcio Costa, collaborating with him on the University City project in Rio. In the early 1940s, at the suggestion of Mayor Juscelino Kubitschek, Niemeyer designed the well-known complex of the church of São Francisco at Pampulha, Belo Horizonte, which inaugurated a new phase of modern architecture.

Niemeyer was one of the committee of ten internationally famous architects, among them Le Corbusier, which was asked to design the

United Nations Headquarters in New York, completed in 1953.

Though he has been responsible for many remarkable buildings in Europe, Africa and Asia, his most outstanding work is probably his contribution to the new capital of Brazil, inaugurated in 1960, for which he designed the major buildings — described as "a spectacular exercise in pure geometry". The noted anthropologist Darcy Ribeiro has said: "Niemeyer is the only Brazilian whose work will survive to the year 3000". André Malraux described the pillars of the Presidential Palace (Palácio da Alvorada) in Brasília as "the most important architectural feature since the Greek column".

Roberto Burle Marx (1909-1994)

A native of São Paulo, Burle Marx has lived in Rio de Janeiro since 1914. He studied painting in Germany (1928-1929). In 1933 he designed his first garden, at the suggestion of Lúcio Costa, and then participated in the work on the Ministry of Education building (1938). His first exhibition of paintings in Rio (1941) was followed by others in Boston, London, Rome and Naples.

Burle Marx has attained an international reputation as a landscape and garden designer thanks to his work in Pampulha, Aterro in Flamengo, Rio de Janeiro and Brasília. He has received honorary doctorates from the London Royal College of Art and the Hague Royal Academy of Fine Arts.

Jorge Amado de Faria (born 1912)

Born in the 'cocoa belt' of Bahia state, he studied law and traveled around Latin America and the U.S.A. An active left-wing politician, he became a deputy in the Federal Parliament. During a lengthy period of political exile, he traveled widely in Europe and Asia.

The best-known and most frequently translated of contemporary Brazilian novelists, he wrote mostly about his native region and its social problems. His most popular works are *Terras do sem fin* (translated as *The Violent Land*, 1942) and *Gabriela, cravo e canela* (*Gabriella, Cloves and Cinnamon*, 1958). A number of his novels have been serialized on Brazilian television, while Gabriella has also been the subject of several foreign-made films.

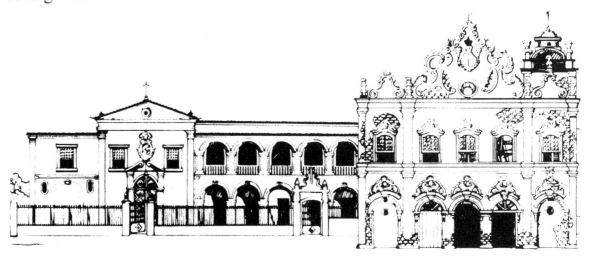

Luis Gonçalves: sketch of the Carmelite monastery in Cachoeira (Bahia). The church, on the right, was begun in 1702.

Important Dates

1500 — Discovery of Brazil by Portuguese navigator Pedro Álvares Cabral.

1530 — Beginning of colonization.

1545 — First exports of sugar.

1549 — Arrival of the first governor general. Founding of the city of Salvador, seat of the governor.

1555 — French invasion of the territory of present-day Rio de Janeiro.
1567

1580 — Brazil under Spanish domination.
1640

1594 — Second French invasion of northeast Brazil (Maranhão).
1615

1616 — Beginning of colonization of Amazonia.

1624 — Dutch invasion of Salvador (Bahia state).
1625

1630 — Dutch colony established in Pernambuco.
1654

1693 — Discovery of gold in Minas Gerais.

1695 — Suppression of the independent 'Black Republic' of Palmares, founded nearly a century earlier by fugitive black slaves.

1700 — Boom years in gold and diamond mining.
1803

1720 — Brazil given the status of a viceroyalty.

1727 — Beginning of the cultivation of coffee.

1759 — Expulsion of the Jesuit order from Brazil.

1763 — Transfer of the capital from Salvador to Rio de Janeiro.

1789 — Conspiracy against Portuguese authorities in Minas Gerais (*Inconfidência Mineíra*): the beginning of the struggle for Brazilian independence.

1799 — Conspiracy in Bahia (*Conjuração Baiana*) to establish a democratic regime in Brazil.

1808 — Arrival of the Portuguese royal family, fleeing Napoleon's troops.

1815 — Proclamation of the United Kingdom of Portugal, Brazil and the Algarves.

1816 — Founding of the Academy of Fine Arts in Rio de Janeiro.

1821 — Return of King John VI to Portugal; his son Pedro appointed prince regent of Brazil.

1822 — Proclamation of the independence of Brazil. Prince regent crowned Emperor Pedro I. Beginning of the Brazilian monarchy.

1824 — Promulgation of Brazil's first constitution.

1831 — Abdication of Pedro I in favor of his minor son, and formation of a provisional regency.

1840 — Pedro de Alcantara becomes Emperor Pedro II at the age of fourteen.

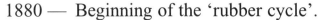

1880 — Beginning of the 'rubber cycle'.

1888 — Decree on the abolition of slavery.

1889 — Proclamation of the Republic.
Pedro II and the royal family leave Brazil.

1897 — Founding of the Brazilian Academy of Letters.

1907 — Brazil participates for the first time in an international conference, the Second International Peace Conference at the Hague.

1910 — Founding of the Service for the Protection of the Indian, directed by General Cândido Rondon, himself of Indian ancestry.

1917 — Brazil declares war on Germany after the sinking of Brazilian merchant ships and thus enters the First World War.

1920 — Beginning of more intensive industrialization in Brazil.

1922 — Modern Art Week in São Paulo.

1929 — Brazil hard hit by the fall in the prices of coffee and raw materials on the world market during the Great Depression.

1930 — Getúlio Vargas, governor of the state of Rio Grande do Sul, assumes power as provisional president. Beginning of the Second Republic.

1942 — Brazil declares war on Germany and its allies after the sinking of Brazilian merchant ships by German submarines.

1944 — Brazilian military contingent fights on the Allied front in Italy.

1945 — President Vargas forced to resign; General Eurico Gaspar Dutra elected President.

1950 — Getúlio Vargas constitutionally elected President of the Republic.

1956 — President Juscelino Kubitschek promotes the development of the
1960 — interior. Brasília is built and inaugurated as the new capital.

1964 — Overthrow of President João Goulart inaugurates 15 years of military rule, with some relaxation of control from 1979.

1982 — Victory of opposition parties at parliamentary elections, November 15. The military regime begins to crumble.

1985 — On the death of President-elect Tancredo Neves, candidate of the united democratic opposition, Vice-President José Sarney becomes President of the Republic.

1988 — New constitution promulgated.

1989 — Fernando Collar de Mello is first president elected by direct vote.

1992 — President Collar, faced with impeachment for corruption, resigns; Vice-President Itamar Franco sworn in to complete his five-year term.

1994 — Election of President Fernando Henrique Cardoso, world-renowned social scientist, formerly Minister of Foreign Affairs and Finance Minister.

Index

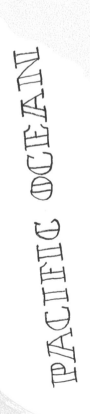

PACIFIC OCEAN

NORTH
ATLANTIC
OCEAN

PACIFIC OCEAN

BRAZIL

SOUTH
ATLANTIC
OCEAN

MANAUS

BELO

RI
S

PO